red Meats and Grilled Sausage • Bu

t Some Roots • Toss Together Some Old Bread • Make Some Grains •

"The only rule in *Cooking for Good Times* is . . . there are no rules. This book and I were destined to be BFFs. While I wish I could pack a rucksack and run away to Paul Kahan's Wisconsin cabin for a summer of salumi and smoked whitefish pizza, I'm glad to have his book to turn to any time I need to feel restored. Welcoming and without pretense, like all great Midwestern fellas, Paul Kahan brings home another culinary hit."

—**CHRISTINA TOSI**, founder/owner of Milk Bar and author of *All About Cake*

Melt Some Cheese • Make Some Pizza Dough • Roast

COOKING for GOOD TIMES

COOKING for GOOD TIMES

super delicious, super simple

paul kahan

with perry hendrix
and rachel holtzman

PHOTOGRAPHS BY PEDEN+MUNK

LORENA JONES BOOKS
An imprint of TEN SPEED PRESS
California | New York

IN LOVING MEMORY
OF RICKY

CONTENTS

SHARING FOOD WE LIKE

WITH PEOPLE WE LIKE

WHEN I STARTED THINKING ABOUT what I wanted to do for my second book—long before the first book was close to done—I kept coming back to what had been the inspiration for my restaurant avec. There was something about that place that had been a part of my life beyond my work that I wanted to somehow translate. In the beginning, before avec became avec, we just wanted a little wine bar next to Blackbird to make some money off the wine. But the food was so good, it ended up being about the wine *and* super-delicious, super-straightforward, super-shareable dishes. And that's really what it's about at its core—avec = with. Whenever someone hasn't been in to eat and wants to know what kind of restaurant avec is, I tell them that it's kind of like the best dinner party everyone wishes they could have—there's great music, tons of wine, and the food just keeps coming out in waves, all served family style. There's really no designation between appetizers and entrées—you don't need to have the charred asparagus salad first and there's no reason you can't eat our signature "deluxe" focaccia with Taleggio cheese alongside your main course.

And while some people like to label our food as European or Mediterranean, I'll be the first to tell you that avec is an American restaurant. Avec chef Perry Hendrix and I are two Midwestern boys making food in the Midwest. All of our ingredients come from the region, or ideally as close to here as possible. But we also like adding ingredients that contribute great flavor, such as za'atar or sumac or harissa. We don't necessarily do things the way someone's grandmother did it, and our muhammara might not be the most traditional one there is, but nothing's off-limits. And nothing is overworked. The food itself is simple; there's not one dish coming out of the kitchen that takes longer than three or four minutes once the order goes in. Just like when you're cooking at home, everything is prepped in advance, and many of our staple (and most well-known) dishes—brined and braised pork shoulder, whole roasted fish, marinated roasted beets—are based on the same tried-and-true methods that we've been using since we opened, with the addition of maybe three or four different components (vinaigrettes, aiolis, and other schmears, spreads, and crunchy things) that get adjusted with the seasons. It's completely about getting friends together and sharing a great meal, not tweaky food.

But this book isn't about avec the restaurant; it's about avec the idea. And the idea that inspired avec and its communal, convivial vibe started with my wife, Mary. Before I had the honor of calling her my wife, or even my girlfriend, Mary was in a horrible motorcycle accident in Le Mans, France. (Hang in there; there's a good payoff coming!) The story didn't start there, though. It started with Mary sitting outside of her office on South Michigan Avenue, eating her lunch. A guy walked up and introduced himself—his name was Jürg Frehner, and he was traveling around the United States. They got to talking, and over the course of the few weeks that he was in Chicago, he and Mary met up, went out for drinks, and she showed him around. (Luckily he had a serious girlfriend and this was truly platonic—or things would have turned out really different for me. . . .)

When it was time for Jürg to leave, he invited Mary to come see him in Europe and bike around France. So fast-forward to Le Mans, where he and Mary were hit head-on by a truck, sustained very serious injuries, and were medevaced to a hospital in Gais, Switzerland—a little cow town in the Swiss Alps near the Austrian border where Jürg had family. Mary convalesced there for about six weeks, healing from a broken arm and hoping to continue her journey. She ended up meeting a woman named Verena, who had just returned to town, was between jobs, and whose partner was in the military as part of his mandatory service. She had nothing to do, and Mary had nothing to do, so the two of them would go out and get into trouble (but not too much trouble), drinking at the *bierstube* and hanging out with Verena's friends (who have since become our very close friends and have intermarried with our friends from the States, leading to an unprecedented Chicago-Gais connection).

Not long after Mary came back to Chicago, she met me. At the time I was working for Erwin Drechsler at Metropolis Café, and he eventually agreed to send me to Europe for my first-ever trip. So as our starting point, Mary decided she would take me back to Switzerland to visit Verena.

It was 10:30 AM on a Sunday when Verena picked us up at the Zurich airport, but she still had a bottle of Champagne for us to drink while she drove the two and a half hours in a snowstorm back to Gais. Within an hour of getting back to her house—a four-hundred-year-old farmhouse with a beautiful wine cellar in the barn, to hold all the great wine she and her partner loved to bring back from Italy, and a big, wood-burning oven in the kitchen—a parade of people started to pour in. It turns out we were about to majorly benefit from two Swiss traditions. The first tradition was that Sundays were for visiting. People all over the town would wander between the houses—sometimes for miles through forests and multiple feet of snow—just to socialize, share a little spread of food, and drink some wine. The second was that, in order to help visitors beat their jet lag, hosts would arrange for people to come over every couple of hours to visit. This also involved eating and drinking wine.

Over the course of our first afternoon there, about thirty people must have come by and, between arrivals, Verena and her partner would refresh the wine, of which we must have gone through fifteen, twenty, bottles. We were also pulling delicious, simple dishes from the oven, plunking them down on the table right in the pots they'd been cooking in. We sliced off hunks of bread, toasted them until they were this side of charred, rubbed 'em with garlic, and put them out for people to top off with cured meats and all the condiments in tubes that the Swiss can't get enough of. (Seriously, their mustards and mayo and relishes and this Marmite-type stuff all come in tubes.) That's where the seed was planted for avec. It's where the seed was planted for how I cook now whenever I host people at my own home. And it's ultimately the foundation of this book.

This book is dedicated to the few truths I've discovered about cooking, especially at home:

You're going to be the most successful if you have a small repertoire of can't-miss dishes, and small changes you can make to them.

You want to make as much as possible in advance (the more you do ahead, the more opportunity there is for having a good time).

There's no order food needs to be served in and no set menu you need to create or follow (one dish plus a beautiful green salad is absolutely a meal).

There's no particular kind of wine you need to serve (even though I'll point you in the right direction because a little extra thought is only going to make things taste that much better).

Your food can absolutely go straight from the oven to a trivet on the table; let it sit for a few minutes while you relax, then eat.

A majority of the chapters in this book will focus on one "master" recipe. This is where you nail the technique—you learn how to make the perfect pizza dough and the most balanced panzanella (there is a 100 percent correct technique when it comes to making bread salad), cook a steak without fear (whether it's flank, strip, rib eye—we'll get you there), and roast the chicken to end all roast chickens (our recipe is a mutation of Joël Robuchon's grandmother's recipe—best yard bird EVER). From there, it's just a matter of what you add—components that mostly can be made in advance will dress up the dish according to whatever season you're in and could also be served on their own. Maybe your roasted and marinated beets get charred and topped with smoked yogurt and crispy lentils (a dish people lose their minds over) or they could get used in a cold dish (tossed with orange, feta, olives, and an olive brine vinaigrette, for example). You could cook orzo and clams into the braising liquid of your pork shoulder and finish it off with fresh peas. Or go with couscous

and braised apricots. You can cook up a big batch of grains—quinoa, farro, basmati rice, you name it—and, depending on what time of year it is, toss them with charred cauliflower and orange segments, or maybe some roasted corn and peaches. Then you pick a small assortment of dishes and you're done. It could be one big dish and two small. Or three or four salads and a dip—you don't always need a big hunk of meat. There's also no such thing as too much food. Most of these recipes are written for six with the idea that they're perfect for four with leftovers.

We're also going to talk about things to eat while cooking—a critical part, and some would argue the whole point, of getting together. You can't underestimate great Spanish smoked oysters with crackers or a batch of the now-sacred avec-style bacon-wrapped, chorizo-stuffed dates. You serve this stuff while you're finishing up dinner and everyone's hanging out in the kitchen having a drink. Maybe toast up some bread and, boom, dinner's started.

This book is also my way of capturing the spirit of one of my favorite places in the world: my cabin in Presque Isle, Wisconsin, a lake town at the very top of the state, about ten minutes south of Michigan's Upper Peninsula. It has become a super-special respite from the city and work demands, where Mary and I can unhook from cell service and Wi-Fi and spend our time surrounded by the quiet of largely unspoiled wilderness. There are about six hundred people who live there year-round, and there's not much more to the place than a handful of roadside restaurants and a sprinkling of houses dotted around almost a thousand (seriously) lakes filled with muskie, walleye, pike, and bass. While a big portion of our days is spent outside—fishing, canoeing, walking in the hemlock forests, fishing some more—another big portion is dedicated to eating and drinking, especially with people we love. Good food and wine nourishes my soul just as much as all that beautiful scenery, but spending the whole day in the kitchen is not what it's all about. It's finding that pretty incredible sweet spot when you're relaxing and eating and enjoying each other's company, sipping on some session beer, rosé, or peasanty, old-world wines (or, when the leaves start to turn, hard cider). That, to me, is the ethos of this whole book. It's preparing a meal in the least complicated way possible, using methods that let you do the little bit of necessary work ahead of time, putting up food that's super-duper tasty, and, most important, enjoying the company and the surroundings.

Speaking of wine (and beer, and in some cases, spirits), throughout the book we've included some of our favorite things to drink with what we're eating. I personally like to offer a few things: There's usually a rosé, a session beer (Tecate, Miller High Life, or, when a little hops are necessary, Founders All Day IPA), and a mix of wines that range from inexpensive to a little more special—but that's just me, a cheffy wine person. I truly believe that a super-gnarly, barn-yardy Rhône wine is every bit as good as your more expensive options. My suggestions, plus those of avec founding father and wine guy, Eduard Seitan, aren't necessarily specific to a region, and they're definitely not going to send you chasing after one particular bottle that'll make or break the meal in your mind. These are just so you can walk into any wine shop and say, "Hey, I'm looking for a light-bodied red or a dry rosé." Done.

The recipes in this book don't have to be made with military precision. There isn't an ingredient here that you can't buy at your neighborhood place. Will you have to cook? Yes, that's part of the deal. But by the time you have people over, it should feel like you're just setting things out or warming things up. There's no split-second timing. There should be no sweating. This is just my way of helping you have a little more fun and drink a little more wine.

But by no means am I recommending that you buy a specific wine or beer to pair with a specific dish. Buy two, four, six bottles or six-packs. Open 'em up and let people enjoy themselves.

Let's face it, whenever people come over to eat, everyone congregates in the kitchen. You could have a beautiful, super-comfortable living room, but everyone always ends up huddled around the kitchen counter, drinking wine and helping put the meal together. So the idea of having stuff that you can do really simply right before your guests get there, while dinner cooks (or in the case of brandade, the night before), is what this chapter is about. At avec, we have a big vat of marinated olives on the counter that we scoop into a dish and throw out for people to snack on while they're deciding what to eat. When I have people over, it's the same thing—I set out some food for them to pick at while we wait for dinner to be ready. One of the inspirations for these kinds of recipes came from Gabrielle Hamilton. She does a super-simple dish with just Parmesan, anchovies, celery, lemon juice, and olive oil as something to nosh on while you're cooking. Bingo. It doesn't get more perfect than that.

I may have a tendency to overdo things, but I say no matter how many people are coming over, pick two or three of these recipes to make and at least one thing that's served with bread. Supplementing that with a plate of nice prosciutto or salami goes without saying. Or pick a recipe or two from chapter 2 (Add Some Cured Meats and Grilled Sausage). Or make a whole meal out of these first two chapters—who doesn't want to eat that way? There are no rules.

MAKE SOME FOOD TO EAT WHILE YOU COOK

To Drink

Pour anything with bubbles, anything that's pink, really whatever is delicious and light on the palate that gets you salivating and ready to eat something a little salty (which describes most of the recipes in this chapter).

Honorable mentions go to:

- Pét Nat (Pétillant Naturel) because it's lower in alcohol and a little tamer than sparkling
- A crisp, clean beer like a pilsner, lager, or session ale (nothing too hoppy or high in alcohol or it'll clobber your palate)
- Provençal rosé
- Spanish white vermouth (so cool and spicy, but the Italians do a good job, too—serve it on ice with a swath of citrus peel)
- anything light and bubbly from Greece, Italy, and France—though this isn't the time for heady Champagne.

The Champagne of beers, Miller High Life, is always an option.

MARINATED OLIVES

We started making these at avec out of necessity—we were getting so slammed that we needed something to drop on the table with the bread to buy us a little time when we got behind in the kitchen. So we got some high-quality olives, drained the liquid, and marinated them in oil, citrus rinds, herbs, and fennel seeds. They're virtually indestructible, so you can keep them, covered, in a cool place for pretty much forever and then you not only have this incredible flavored olive oil to use in vinaigrettes or drizzle over bread, but you also have the makings of a Holy Shit moment when you present a table full of hungry people with them alongside some warm bread. It's a nice mopping-up moment. It's the same at home if you keep a batch in your fridge. I'm partial to olives that still have their pits—Picholine, Niçoise, Lucques—because they don't get all mushy like most pitted ones, and while they're a little bit more work to eat, they're a great activity while having some wine and waiting for whatever's next.

2 cups mixed olives with pits
1 cup extra-virgin olive oil
Zest and juice of 1 orange
1 sprig rosemary, leaves stripped
   from the stem

2 fresh bay leaves*
2 teaspoons fennel seeds, toasted
   in a skillet until aromatic
1 teaspoon crushed red chile flakes

14

MARINATE THE OLIVES Drain the brine from the olives and rinse them under warm water to remove more of the brine. In a medium bowl, combine the drained olives with the oil, orange zest and juice, the rosemary, bay leaves, fennel seeds, and chile flakes. Let the olives marinate at room temperature or in the fridge for at least 1 hour and up to forever.

SERVE OR STORE Serve the olives at room temperature or straight out of the fridge. Return any leftovers to the fridge, where you can store them until they run out.

*If you only have dried bay leaves, just leave them out.

CHARRED MARKET PEPPERS WITH PICKLED FETA

MAKES 6 SERVINGS

For this one, you take just about any pepper you find at the market, sweet or hot—shishitos, Jimmy Nardellos (my favorite), Fresnos, sweet Hungarian wax, or cayenne—toss 'em with olive oil and salt, and grill 'em on a hot grill or sear them in a hot pan. The peppers turn into these little time bombs that fill up with this hot pepper juice that bleeds out—when you carefully cut into them after cooking, hence time bombs—and mixes with the brininess of the pickled feta and makes what's essentially nature's vinaigrette.

Pickled Feta

1 cup white wine vinegar
1 sprig fresh mint, 1 mint tea bag, or
    ½ teaspoon dried mint
1 teaspoon sugar
1 teaspoon kosher salt
¼ teaspoon crushed red chile flakes
½ cup water
8-ounce block feta cheese

Charred Peppers

¼ cup extra-virgin olive oil
1 pound sweet peppers (of all colors),
    seeds removed and cut into
    ½-inch strips
8 ounces slightly hot chiles (shishitos,
    Jimmy Nardellos, Fresnos, sweet
    Hungarian wax, cayenne)
1 teaspoon kosher salt
1 tablespoon sherry vinegar or
    red wine vinegar

MAKE THE PICKLED FETA In a small pot, combine the white wine vinegar, mint, sugar, salt, chile flakes, and water and bring to a simmer over medium-high heat. Remove from the heat and let the mixture cool completely.

Place the feta in a glass (or other nonreactive) container and pour in the pickling liquid. Cover and let sit in the refrigerator for 1 hour before serving. The pickled feta can made up to 1 week ahead and stored in the fridge.

CHAR THE PEPPERS In a large cast-iron skillet over high heat, add the oil, peppers and chiles in a single layer, and the salt. Cook without stirring for about 4 minutes, or until the peppers are blistered and charred. If necessary, cook in two batches. Add the sherry or red wine vinegar.

SERVE OR STORE Crumble the pickled feta over the top and serve. The peppers can be stored for up to 1 week in the refrigerator and tossed back in a 300°F oven for 5 minutes to reheat before serving.

YOU PICK A VEGETABLE! (WITH OLIVE OIL, ANCHOVIES, AND HARD CHEESE)

MAKES 6 SNACK SERVINGS

This is thievery of Gabrielle Hamilton's celery, anchovy, and Parmesan dish. Hers is basically just shaved celery, celery leaves, really-good-quality Parm in big crumbles—between the size of a nickel and a quarter—and a lot of olive oil. I can't think of anything I'd rather eat, to be honest. This basic combination is pretty much unbeatable and works with a bunch of vegetables, cooked or raw—fava beans, fennel, radishes, chicories, thinly shaved cauliflower or broccoli, celery root, turnips, tomatoes, zucchini or summer squash, peppers. Pretty much everything. As for cheese, there's a lot of bad Parmesan out there, which sucks because it's kind of expensive. The only ones to use are Grana Padano, Parmigiano-Reggiano, or the greatest of them all, Vacche Rosse (the original Parmigiano-Reggiano from the milk of red cows).

1 pound raw vegetable of your choice, such as fava beans, radishes, celery, fennel, or tomatoes
¼ cup extra-virgin olive oil
1 teaspoon lemon zest
Juice of 1 lemon
6 anchovy fillets, rinsed if salt-packed

2-ounce block Parmigiano or other hard salty cheese
6 to 10 cranks black pepper
1 loaf warm crusty bread, such as ciabatta (see page 44) or sourdough, sliced

PREP YOUR VEG Slice the vegetables thinly—⅛ inch thick for the radishes, ¼ inch for the celery and fennel, and ⅓ inch for the tomatoes.

SERVE Place your vegetables on a rimmed serving plate. Drown in the olive oil. Add the lemon zest and juice, then tear the anchovy fillets into 3 or 4 pieces and scatter them over the top. Using a vegetable peeler (we like the Y-shaped one), cut shards from the cheese or just crumble with your hands. Toss the cheese over the top of the vegetables and then finish with the black pepper. Serve with the bread, using it as a vehicle or a mop, or both.

Buying Olive Oil

We should pretty much sell this book with jugs of olive oil because you'll go through so much making these recipes. What can I say? They're soppers. There are really only a few things that make the difference between how something is cooked in a restaurant and how things are usually done at home, and the quality and amount of olive oil used is one of the differences. (Along with using a high enough heat on the stove, making sure there's enough acid in a dish, and using a nice amount of—but not too much—salt.) I think Americans get a little hung up on the oil factor—they think it might make something too greasy. But olive oil adds a lot of flavor (and can also add acidity, if it's spicy), which is why we're going big here. In the beginning it's probably going to feel like more than you're comfortable using, and if you want to do it to your liking instead, that's fine. But push yourself because it's all about swabbing up those juices afterward.

The kind of olive oil you use is just as important as any other ingredient you buy. Personally, I look first at region. I think a lot of the Tuscan olive oils end up being a little too bitter and peppery to use a ton of. And the Greek oils can be super-buttery and heavy on the palate. I always look for Spanish varietals, Arbequina in particular. It's got a nice grassiness and acidity to it, almost more like a green apple, and it's a little leaner than heavier varieties.

Dates by Bob (aka Mary's Dad)

When I was about seventy, right before I retired, I said to my wife, Mary, "You've been cooking for nine people (us two and our seven children) all of these years; I think I'm going to try to take some of that burden off of you." So I started cooking. I got pretty interested in it, too—I'd look on the Internet for recipes and had subscriptions to *Gourmet* magazine and *Cook's Illustrated* and watched cooking shows, and I remember seeing a stuffed date recipe (though I couldn't recall from where) and thought, *That sounds interesting*. At first I used store-bought chorizo but didn't like it because it wasn't hot enough, so I would make my own that had enough kick. My father made Polish sausage, and he passed that on to me, so I started with that. I thought, *Hey, I know the basics of making pork sausage*, and I researched the herbs and spices that go into chorizo instead of the traditional marjoram for Polish sausage or fennel for Italian sausage. And then I discovered Medjool dates, which are so much juicier than the smaller, drier ones from the grocery store. I'd make these for pretty much everything, and they were always a big hit. And when Paul and my daughter Mary came over sometime and had 'em, Paul took them over, and that's been that.

BACON-WRAPPED, CHORIZO-STUFFED DATES

MAKES 8 SERVINGS

PICTURED ON PAGE 21. I first had these dates when Mary's dad, Bob, brought them to one of the epic Christmas parties that we used to throw every year for the restaurants' staffs (until we were going through about fourteen kegs of beer and staying up all night smoking and pulling twelve pork shoulders—then we called it quits). I knew from the moment I tasted one that there was a place on our menu for them. I kept bugging avec's original chef, Koren Grieveson, during our first week, saying "We gotta put these on, gotta put these on," and her answer, every time, was "no." Actually, it was [expletive expletive] . . . but she finally agreed and—with the addition of the piquillo-tomato sauce—the dates have been on offer at avec ever since. The recipe hasn't changed at all in fifteen years. We've had the same guy makin' 'em, too—Jorge Ruiz. From the very beginning he's been cranking out more than three hundred a day, five days a week; that's almost two mil to date. He's made nearly every stuffed date at the restaurant—no kidding. When he goes on vacation he fills up the freezer with them because when someone covered for him once, people complained that the dates weren't the same. He's even developed his own chorizo blend that's spicy enough to offset the sweetness of the dates. He throws in beef scraps, pork scraps, prosciutto scraps—whatever we have around. You get more bang for your buck that way and they taste better. I get the bug from time to time and say let's just take them off—I'm tired of them—but there are some things you just can't touch. People would riot.

1 tablespoon extra-virgin olive oil
8 cloves garlic, thinly sliced
8 small shallots, thinly sliced
8 ounces (about 1 cup) roasted piquillo peppers with any jar juices, or any roasted red peppers plus juices*
2 cups whole peeled canned tomatoes plus juices

Kosher salt
Freshly ground black pepper
16 Medjool dates, pitted
8 ounces fresh (uncured) chorizo sausage, casings removed**
8 slices bacon

continued

23

*You can find jarred piquillo peppers in most grocery stores. If you can't find them, substitute roasted red peppers.
**Make sure to buy uncured, fresh chorizo sausage for this, not the salami-like cured kind.

BACON-WRAPPED, CHORIZO-STUFFED DATES

continued

MAKE THE SAUCE Heat the oil in a medium saucepan over medium heat. Add the garlic and shallots and cook until tender, about 5 minutes. Add the peppers and tomatoes, gently breaking up the tomatoes with a spoon, and bring to a simmer. Decrease the heat to low and cook for 30 minutes, until the liquid in the sauce has mostly evaporated. Season with salt and pepper.

Let the sauce cool slightly, then transfer it to a blender and blend until smooth. Thin with warm water, if necessary. You want it to be thick but not so thick that it mounds on the plate.

PREP AND COOK THE DATES Preheat the oven to 350°F. Stuff the dates with the chorizo, using about 1 tablespoon of chorizo per date. Cut the bacon slices in half lengthwise and wrap a slice around each date. Arrange the dates on a small baking sheet and bake for 15 to 20 minutes, or until the chorizo is cooked through. Preheat the broiler. Broil the dates for 2 to 4 minutes, until the bacon is dark brown and crisp.

SERVE Spread the sauce over a serving plate and place the dates over the top. Serve warm.

BRANDADE

You could call this spread by its fancy given name (pronounced *brahn-DAHD*), or just call it "warm potato, garlic, and salted fish dip." We opened avec with this on the menu. Day One-ski, man. Namely because I love salt cod in every way, shape, and form (along with every old-world wine country—Italy, France, Spain; there's your trilogy of wine greatness). It's also stupid easy for a restaurant pick up—you're basically just pureeing the fish and potatoes into a garlicky glop, which you can make ahead of time, then scooping it into a pan with cream and olive oil to heat it through. The important thing to point out, though, is that this is more akin to super-bubbly, rich mashed potatoes or a potato dip than anything fish-like. The fish just adds some saltiness and sort of umami flavor to it. All you need is a good soft bread, like ciabatta, that's toasted with olive oil, and you spoon all that action over it. Easy to make, easier to share.

The brandade base can be kept in your refrigerator for up to five days or even frozen in smaller amounts. You'll end up with about 2 cups, so freeze in 1-cup batches and you can just defrost in the fridge overnight and toss into another round of brandade.

The only quasi-fussy thing here is buying the salt cod, but you can order it online and it can sit in your cupboard for six months. It's pretty indestructible.

8 ounces salt cod, soaked in water
    overnight in your refrigerator
    and drained
2 cups whole milk
8 ounces Yukon gold potatoes, peeled
6 cloves garlic, peeled
1 tablespoon unsalted butter, melted

1 cup heavy cream
1 teaspoon freshly ground
    black pepper
2 tablespoons extra-virgin olive oil
1 tablespoon sliced chives
2 cranks black pepper

MAKE THE BASE In a large saucepan, combine the salt cod and milk. Bring to a simmer over medium-low heat and cook until the fish is tender and falling apart, about 30 minutes. Drain the milk and discard it.

While the fish is cooking, place the potatoes in a large saucepan and cover with cold water. Bring to a simmer over medium-high heat and cook until the potatoes are tender, about 20 minutes. Drain. In the bowl of a food processor, combine the potatoes, cod, garlic, butter, ½ cup of the cream, and pepper. Process until the mixture is well combined and smooth. It'll be thick!

FINISH THE DIP AND SERVE In a small saucepan, combine the cod mixture with the remaining ½ cup cream and the oil. Place over medium heat and cook, whisking occasionally, until hot and creamy, about 5 minutes. Serve in a bowl topped with the chives and pepper.

BEET AND WALNUT DIP

This is essentially a muhammara, a pretty traditional Middle Eastern spread. It's usually made with roasted peppers, but we do it with roasted beets because you get more of an earthiness with that same roasty flavor thanks to roasting the beets, marinating them, and then charring them—like taking a beet salad and tossing it in a crushing hot pan. It's something we'll get into more in chapter 4 (along with why you shouldn't be afraid of beets, 'cause they're delicious), but this basically brings out all of the beets' natural sugars and caramelizes them. Then they get tossed with some day-old bread (something we're always trying to use up in one form or another), olive oil, lemon juice, chile, garlic, and pomegranate molasses (or balsamic or saba) and buzzed in a blender. Serve it with good crackers (like the Seed Crackers on page 40, or store-bought crackers) and you're good.

1 cup leftover roasted and marinated beets (see page 84)

½ cup raw walnuts

¼ cup bread crumbs (from 1 slice artisan-style bread, such as ciabatta, toasted and torn into pieces)

1 clove garlic, peeled

1 teaspoon ground Urfa chile, or ¼ teaspoon crushed red chile flakes

¼ teaspoon smoked paprika

1½ tablespoons freshly squeezed lemon juice

3 tablespoons extra-virgin olive oil

1½ teaspoons pomegranate molasses, aged balsamic vinegar (the thick syrupy kind), or saba

1 teaspoon kosher salt

⅓ cup water

Grilled bread, crackers, butter lettuce cups, or cut vegetables for serving

ROAST THE BEETS, ETC. Preheat the broiler. Arrange the beets, walnuts, and bread crumbs on a rimmed baking sheet. Place under the broiler and cook until the nuts and bread are toasted and starting to char, 4 to 6 minutes.

FINISH THE DIP Transfer the lot to a food processor or blender along with the garlic, Urfa chile, paprika, lemon juice, oil, pomegranate molasses, salt, and water. Process until the mixture is smooth but still with a bit of texture, about 1 minute. Transfer to a serving bowl.

SERVE OR STORE Serve with good crackers, butter lettuce cups, or fresh veggies or store in the fridge for up to 5 days.

Beet Nextovers

This recipe is a great way to use up leftover roasted and marinated beets. But if you don't have those handy, you could make a fresh batch with two large beets. Just coat with olive oil, salt, and pepper; wrap 'em in foil; and roast at 350°F until tender, about 1 hour.

CHARRED SUMMER SQUASH–SESAME DIP

MAKES 6 SERVINGS

We're always pushing the edge of charred-not-burnt with our vegetables to get those extra layers of flavor, such as in baba ghanoush, which is essentially burnt eggplant. For this recipe, we take whole summer squash instead (or halved, if they're baseball bats), rub 'em with spices, char 'em, and puree them with just a little olive oil, lemon juice, and tahini. We really like Soom tahini, a Michael Solomonov staple that's made out of sesame seeds that are sourced by a group of sisters from Philadelphia. The best way to know what kind you like best is trial and error—it should be smooth, rich, and not bitter.

2 pounds summer squash, such as zucchini, patty pan, zephyr, or yellow
2 tablespoons extra-virgin olive oil
1 teaspoon kosher salt
1 tablespoon za'atar (or 1 teaspoon each dried oregano, sumac, and sesame seeds) or ½ teaspoon crushed red chile flakes

2 tablespoons freshly squeezed lemon juice
¼ cup tahini
Seed Crackers (page 40), store-bought crackers, or pita wedges for serving

ROAST THE SQUASH Prepare a medium-hot grill or preheat the broiler to high. Season the squash with 1 tablespoon of the oil, the salt, and spice of choice. If grilling, carefully lay the squash over the hottest part of the grill. Cook on one side until the squash is well charred and tender, about 3 minutes. If using a broiler, arrange the squash on a rimmed baking sheet and place it as close to the broiler as you can. Cook on one side until the squash is deeply charred and tender, about 3 minutes, and set aside to cool.

FINISH THE DIP Once the squash has cooled slightly, chop it into chunks, and transfer it to a blender or food processor. Add the remaining 1 tablespoon oil and the lemon juice and tahini. Blend until the squash is completely smooth, about 3 minutes. If the mixture doesn't want to move, splash in a couple teaspoons of water.

SERVE OR STORE Serve with crackers or pita wedges or store in the fridge for up to 5 days.

PERFECT HUMMUS

Our Perfect Hummus is pretty much the product of our quest to replicate Michael Solomonov's at Zahav in Philadelphia. After a lot of failed attempts to get that same insanely rich creaminess, we eventually got a recipe thanks to Lior Lev Sercarz (of the unofficial Israeli mafia and our go-to spice-blend master to whom we wrote a love letter in *Cheers to the Publican*). We discovered that success was owed to two things: starting with really good tahini (and more of it than most people are used to adding to hummus) and understanding how to treat chickpeas right. The secret is soaking the chickpeas overnight with a fair amount of baking soda, draining off the water, baking the chickpeas with more baking soda on top, then submerging them in cold water while you aggressively massage off the skins and skim them off the top—that's how you produce super-silky hummus. After that, the chickpeas basically get cooked to death and then pureed with an already-pureed mixture of tahini, lemon juice, and garlic—a Solomonov trick to get all the garlic flavor without the acrid heat. It really is the perfect hummus.

But when Perry was cooking for the Pitchfork Music Festival one summer and had to make about twenty-five gallons of hummus or some obscene amount close to that, he knew there was no way he'd be able to prep, like, fifty pounds of chickpeas. That's when Cheater Hummus was born (see the next recipe for that version).

1 pound dried chickpeas
2 tablespoons baking soda
1 tablespoon plus 2 teaspoons kosher
    salt, plus more as needed
1¼ cups freshly squeezed lemon juice
9 cloves garlic, unpeeled
1¾ cups tahini*
⅔ cup ice water

*The quality of tahini that you use makes a difference. Go ahead and order Soom tahini. You're welcome.

SOAK THE CHICKPEAS The night before you want to serve the hummus, in a large sealable container, combine the chickpeas, 1 tablespoon of the baking soda, and enough water to cover by at least 4 inches. Set aside in a cool dark spot (or refrigerate).

COOK THE CHICKPEAS The next day, preheat the oven to 400°F. Drain the chickpeas and spread them in a single layer on a rimmed baking sheet. Dust the chickpeas with the remaining 1 tablespoon baking soda and bake for 15 minutes. Transfer the chickpeas to a large bowl and cover with cold water. Massage the chickpeas aggressively until the skins slip off and float to the surface. Remove the skins with a slotted spoon or small fine-mesh strainer and discard. Try to remove as many skins as you can; this will get you the creamiest hummus.

Drain the chickpeas and transfer them to a stockpot. Cover them with water by 3 inches. Bring to a boil over medium-high heat, decrease the heat to low, and cook until the chickpeas are incredibly tender, about 45 minutes. Cook longer if needed, adding more water if the level dips below the surface of the chickpeas. Remove the pot from the heat and stir in 1 tablespoon of the salt. Let the chickpeas sit for 5 minutes, then drain them, reserving the cooking liquid.

FINISH THE HUMMUS While the chickpeas are cooling, in a blender, combine the lemon juice and garlic. Blend on high speed until obliterated, about 2 minutes. Let the mixture sit for about 30 minutes, then strain, reserving the liquid and discarding any solids.

In the bowl of a stand mixer, combine the tahini, ice water, the 2 teaspoons salt, and 1 cup plus 2 tablespoons of the garlic–lemon juice. Mix on low speed until creamy, about 3 minutes.

In a blender, combine 1½ cups of the cooked chickpeas with 1 cup of the prepared tahini, plus ¼ cup of the chickpea cooking liquid. Blend on high speed until creamy. Add more of the cooking liquid to achieve the desired consistency, if necessary.

Dump out the contents of the blender into a large bowl and, working in batches, repeat with the remaining chickpeas and tahini. You will ultimately add all of the chickpeas and tahini to the hummus mixture, so don't worry if some batches are slightly smaller or larger than others. Mix together the batches of hummus, and taste. It might need a bit more salt. And if it's too thick, stir in more of the chickpea cooking water, a tablespoon or so at a time, until it's the right consistency.

SERVE OR STORE Serve the hummus at room temperature. Store in an airtight container in the fridge for up to 5 days.

CHEATER HUMMUS

MAKES 2 CUPS

Here's Perry's hummus hack: He figured out that by using canned chickpeas, tossing in the chickpeas' liquid, and again, adding more tahini than most people think is a good idea, he got pretty damn close to the original. When I came in to taste it and he told me that it wasn't the original—that he used canned—I didn't believe him. It was almost, *almost*, as good. Maybe a *tick* not as good. But still super-freaking good.

1 (15.5-ounce) can chickpeas*
¼ cup tahini
Juice of ½ lemon

½ teaspoon kosher salt
½ teaspoon ground cumin
1 teaspoon extra-virgin olive oil

MAKE THE HUMMUS Pour off ¼ cup of the liquid from the chickpeas and pour the remaining chickpeas and liquid into a blender or food processor. Add the tahini, lemon juice, salt, and cumin. Blend or process on high until very smooth. Do not be afraid to run your blender or food processor for a long time (like 2 to 3 minutes). This is where the creaminess comes from. While the machine is running, add the oil in a thin drizzle.

SERVE OR STORE Serve the hummus at room temperature. Store in an airtight container in the fridge for up to 5 days.

*I like the Goya brand; you can find it in most supermarkets in the Mexican foods aisle.

SALMON ESCABECHE
WITH LEMON MAYO

MAKES 6 SERVINGS

All you're doing here is partially cooking salmon until it's medium-rare, pouring over a vinaigrette—whose acid finishes the "cooking"—and smashing it all on some bread with a schmear of mayo.

Lemon Mayo

1 cup store-bought mayonnaise*
Zest and juice of 1 lemon
1 clove garlic, grated or minced
¼ teaspoon kosher salt
2 cranks black pepper

Salmon

¼ teaspoon ground cumin
½ teaspoon ground coriander
¼ teaspoon ground fennel seeds
2 teaspoons kosher salt

1 pound salmon fillet, bones
  removed**
1 small red onion, thinly sliced
1 small Fresno or jalapeño chile,
  seeded and thinly sliced
½ cup extra-virgin olive oil
¼ cup red wine vinegar

1 loaf ciabatta (see page 44),
  sliced***

MAKE THE MAYO In a small bowl, combine the mayonnaise, lemon zest and juice, the garlic, and salt. Garnish with the pepper. Set aside.

COOK THE SALMON In a small bowl, combine the cumin, coriander, fennel seed, and 1 teaspoon of the salt. Rub the flesh side of the salmon with the spice mixture and let it sit in your refrigerator for 1 hour.

Preheat the oven to 300°F. Lightly oil a rimmed baking sheet. Place the salmon on the baking sheet and bake until the fish is tender and just cooked through, 12 to 15 minutes.

While the fish is cooking, in a small bowl, combine the onion, chile, oil, vinegar, and the remaining 1 teaspoon salt. Massage the onion with the oil and vinegar until tender. When the fish is finished cooking, pour the onion mixture over it. Let the fish sit for 15 minutes at room temperature or up to overnight in the fridge (and gently warm before serving).

SERVE Spread slices of bread with a schmear of the mayo and a spoonful of onion-topped salmon, smashed onto the bread.

*I like Hellmann's and Duke's.
**Ask your fishmonger to take care of it.
***Bonus points for oiled, grilled, and rubbed with garlic.

SEED CRACKERS

MAKES ABOUT 4 CUPS

Just like the crust of a really good loaf of ciabatta is the ultimate delivery mechanism for getting more food shoveled into your mouth, the cracker is its esteemed—and arguably superior—counterpart. It's less filling than bread, its scoop-ability is unquestionable, and it's crispy. I have a problem just walking by something crispy and not eating it. These crackers are whole grain and have a ton of seeds on top—flax, sesame, nigella, pumpkin, sunflower. Name a seed; it's on there. But I don't think you have to choose between crackers and bread; I like putting out both because they're each built for something different. Whereas bread is like the mop to soak up stuff on your plate, the cracker is more like an edible spoon. Brandade? Bread. Walnut and Beet Dip? Cracker. Charred Squash Dip? Cracker. Hummus? Either.

Dough

⅓ cup plus 2 tablespoons bread flour, plus more for dusting
⅓ cup rye flour
⅓ cup warm water
1 tablespoon plus 1 teaspoon extra-virgin olive oil
½ teaspoon kosher salt

Seed Mix

½ cup flax seeds
½ cup sesame seeds
¼ cup nigella seeds (aka charnuska)
3 tablespoons pumpkin seeds
3 tablespoons sunflower seeds

Cornmeal or semolina
Kosher salt

MIX THE DOUGH In a large bowl, combine the flours, warm water, oil, and salt and mix until fully incorporated. Let the dough rest, covered with a clean kitchen towel, for 30 minutes.

MIX THE SEEDS In a separate bowl, combine all the seeds and stir until well mixed.

FORM AND BAKE THE CRACKERS Preheat the oven to 325°F with a rack in the middle of the oven, or 300°F if your oven runs hot. Line a baking sheet with parchment paper and dust it with the semolina or cornmeal to prevent the cracker from sticking. Set aside.

Dust a clean surface with a small amount of bread flour. Turn out the dough and lightly dust it with flour. Use a rolling pin to roll out the dough until it fits the baking sheet, about 18 x 12 inches. The dough should be very thin. If your pan is smaller, use less dough so it stays thin enough (and bake the overage on a second lined baking sheet). Lay the dough on the baking sheet and brush with water so the dough is tacky but not incredibly wet. Sprinkle with the desired amount of the seed mix. (I recommend ½ cup of seeds, but it's your cracker, so top with as many or as few as you want.) Save any leftover seed mix in an airtight container to use another time. Lightly sprinkle the cracker with salt and bake for 20 minutes. Rotate the pan 180 degrees and bake for another 10 minutes, or 20 minutes if baking at 300°F. The cracker will be golden brown and very crisp. If the cracker bends when folded, bake for another 5 minutes, or until it doesn't. Let the cracker sheet cool on the pan.

SERVE OR STORE Break the cracker sheet into shards to serve. Store in an airtight container for up to 1 week.

HOMEMADE MATZO WITH CANNED OR SMOKED FISH AND BUTTER

My dad owned a smoked-fish shop called Village Fishery in Rogers Park, Illinois, and he drove a Monte Carlo that I called the "Fishmobile." It was the car he'd drive home from the factory at night, maybe doing a couple deliveries first, so the smoke and oil from the fish just seeped into every corner of that thing. In high school, if I ever wanted to borrow a car to go on a date, he'd say, "You can take the Monte Carlo." It would take me six hours to clean it just so you could sit in it without holding your nose, and inevitably I'd pick the gal up and she'd say, "It smells disgusting in here." Great start. (I didn't go on too many dates.) This isn't related to the recipe so much as a small detour down memory lane, but smoked fish really does have a special place in my heart. And it doesn't get much better than eating it on a cracker with salted, cultured butter. Just about any smoked fish or shellfish works here—cold-smoked salmon, hot-smoked trout, anchovies, mussels, mackerel, sardines, octopus; anything from a can. (Spanish products tend to be the best, followed by Portuguese. Oil-packed, preferably olive oil over other veggie oils.)

The crackers are just water, flour, oil, and a little salt. They get cooked on a pizza stone until crisp, like a lavash, and blistered, like matzo.

41

4 cups all-purpose flour, plus more for dusting
1 tablespoon extra-virgin olive oil
1 teaspoon kosher salt
¾ to 1 cup water

Salted, cured butter, at room temperature
Oil-packed canned sardines (with the chile pepper, if you can find it) or other smoked fish

MAKE THE MATZO Preheat the oven to 500°F. This is a great time to use that pizza stone. If you don't have one, a rimless baking sheet will do. Just put it on the lowest oven rack and let it preheat with the oven. Same goes for the stone.

In a large bowl, combine the flour, oil, and salt. Mix in the water, starting with ¾ cup, adding more a few drops at a time as needed until a dough forms. Alternatively, this dough can be mixed very quickly in a food processor and the results will be the same; I just prefer to do it by hand. Cover and set aside to rest for 20 minutes.

Turn the dough out onto a well-floured surface. Cut the dough into four equal pieces. Use a rolling pin to roll out the dough as thin as you can get it. Alternatively, you could run it through a pasta machine, decreasing the thickness after each pass until you have a very thin dough. Repeat with the remaining pieces of dough.

Trim the dough into 8-inch squares. Prick the dough all over with a fork and then arrange the squares on the pizza stone or baking sheet. Bake for 1 to 2 minutes, until golden and crisp. Transfer the crackers to a cooling rack and set aside until cool to the touch.

SERVE OR STORE Slather the crackers with the butter and top with fish. Store leftover crackers in an airtight container at room temperature indefinitely.

CIABATTA

MAKES 2 LOAVES

This is a great workhorse bread with a neutral flavor that's just as much a vehicle for swabbing up sauce and olive oil and slathering with spreads as it is about great bread. The recipe comes from Greg Wade, head baker at Publican Quality Bread, and it'll get you crisp crust with a fluffy middle that doesn't have too many holes—which you don't want because then all your dip falls through. I do recommend investing in a scale because they're super-cheap and they'll take your bread baking to a better, more streamlined place, but I've also included the cup and spoon measurements if it's not a leap you've made yet.

And remember this: While I'm a big fan of fresh-baked bread—and this recipe will get you there every time—making it isn't necessary for a good meal. Great bread from a local bakery is just fine. Or you can take just-okay bread to the next level by toasting or grilling it with good extra-virgin olive oil (aka EVOO), rubbing it with garlic, and hitting it with some salt.

Pre-ferment
¼ cup / 175 grams bread flour
Pinch of active dry yeast
¾ cup water plus 2 tablespoons /
    175 grams lukewarm water
    (about 80°F)

Soaker
⅓ cup / 45 grams whole-wheat flour
⅓ cup / 45 grams whole rye flour
6 tablespoons plus 1½ teaspoons /
    90 grams lukewarm water
    (about 80°F)

Final Mix
4 cups plus 3 tablespoons /
    650 grams bread flour, plus more
    for sprinkling
2¼ cups / 465 grams lukewarm water
    (about 80°F)
2 tablespoons / 55 grams honey
¼ cup plus 3 tablespoons / 65 grams
    hemp seeds
¾ teaspoon / 3 grams dry yeast
4 teaspoons / 25 grams salt

ON DAY ONE, MAKE THE PRE-FERMENT Combine the bread flour, yeast, and water in a large bowl and mix by hand until fully incorporated. Let the mixture sit in a large airtight container at room temperature (about 72°F) for 12 hours. The dough will double in size.

MAKE THE SOAKER Combine all the ingredients in a large bowl and mix by hand until fully incorporated. Let the mixture sit in a large airtight container at room temperature for 12 hours.

ON DAY TWO, DO THE FINAL MIX Transfer the pre-ferment and soaker to the bowl of a stand mixer fitted with the dough hook attachment. Add the bread flour, lukewarm water, and honey. Mix on the lowest speed for 2 minutes. Stop the mixer and scrape down and beneath the dough with a bowl scraper. Mix for 1 minute more. The dough should be fully mixed with no pockets of flour. Let the dough rest in the bowl of the mixer at room temperature for 15 minutes. Sprinkle the hemp seeds, yeast, and salt over the dough and mix on very low speed for 1 minute. Once they're fully incorporated into the dough, turn the mixer up to speed 5 and mix for 12 minutes, or until the dough is smooth and shiny and pulls away from the sides of the mixing bowl.

DO THE BULK FERMENTATION Remove the bowl from the mixer and cover it. Let the dough ferment for 45 minutes at room temperature, then give the dough its first fold. To do this, scoop your hands underneath each side of the dough and pull the underside up and over the top. Let the dough sit at room temperature in the mixing bowl for another 45 minutes, then fold the dough a second time. Ferment for 1 hour more, or until the dough feels very light and has doubled in volume.

SHAPE THE DOUGH Turn the dough out onto a surface dusted with bread flour. Sprinkle some flour on top of the dough, which will help make it easier to work with. Using a bench scraper, cut the dough in half. Take each half and gently tug it into an 8 x 12-inch rectangle, trying to keep the dough as thick as possible.

Arrange the first dough rectangle on the work surface so that its long side is closest to you. Like you're folding a letter, take the left edge of the dough and fold one-third of it toward the center. Repeat with the right side, folding it over the top of the left side, so you end up with a roughly 5 x 12-inch rectangle. Flour a large kitchen towel. Place the dough seam-side up on the towel. Repeat the process with the second rectangle of dough, then place the folded dough on the towel, leaving 4 inches between the loaves. Pinch the towel between the loaves and pull up so that the loaves are now directly next to each other with a thin piece of fabric separating them. Wrap the ends of the towel around the dough just tightly enough to help the loaves keep their shape. Let the dough rest at room temperature for 1 hour to proof.

BAKE THE LOAVES Preheat the oven to 500°F with a pizza stone and a clay baker or large pot on the middle rack of the oven. Gently place one of the loaves seam-side down directly onto the baking stone. Carefully invert the clay baker or pot over the dough, covering it. Place the remaining loaf of dough, still in the towel, into the fridge while the first loaf bakes. Bake for 20 minutes, then remove the clay baker, but keep the baker in the oven so it can stay hot. Bake for 5 minutes more, or until the bread's crust is deeply browned. Repeat with the second loaf.

SERVE OR STORE Slice the bread when cool to the touch. Store leftover bread in a paper bag at room temperature for up to 3 days.

AVEC DELUXE FOCACCIA

MAKES 2 FOCACCIAS

There's a story here. When I was doing research for avec, a buddy of mine named Michael Schlow—who has a ton of restaurants in Boston and Washington, D.C.—said, "You gotta go to this restaurant in Midtown Manhattan called Da Ciro." He told me to sit at the counter in front of the wood oven and order the Deluxe Focaccia. I saw what Schlow was talking about—the technique was something totally new to me. They roll out the dough, oil it, season it, cook it, dock it (poke a bunch of holes in it), bake it until it's almost done, cut it in half through the middle and fill it with cheese (in their case, a sheep-and-cow's milk Robiola), and then slide it back in the oven to finish baking into melty goodness. So I watched the technique and learned it and, after about a thousand iterations with avec's Koren Grieveson, started using it at avec (but with good-quality ricotta and Taleggio because I wanted something a little lighter . . . and cheaper, if I'm telling the whole story).

Chefs from all over would come into the restaurant during the James Beard Awards weekend, and everyone would come up to the pass to watch our guys split the focaccia because they'd never seen it before. And if anyone who has eaten at avec catches wind that this book is coming out, they'll demand that this recipe be in here because in all honesty, it's really, really special—all doughy and oily with the melty cheese, a fresh herb mix we call "Choppy," and some truffle oil to top it off. It's by far one of the hardest recipes in the book, but man is it a good one. Like the ciabatta recipe, I've also given you the metric measures so you can put that scale to good use. Give it a shot; we'll put Perry's cell phone number in the back of the book in case you need help. Call anytime, day or night.

Dough

2½ cups / 350 grams all-purpose flour, plus more for dusting*
½ teaspoon / 2 grams active dry yeast
¼ cup / 45 grams extra-virgin olive oil
¾ cup plus 1 tablespoon / 180 grams lukewarm water (about 80°F)
1¼ teaspoons / 10 grams kosher salt

Cheese Filling

1 pound fresh whole-milk ricotta cheese
1 tablespoon each chopped fresh parsley, chives, and tarragon (aka Choppy)
4 ounces Taleggio cheese

1 tablespoon extra-virgin olive oil
¾ teaspoon kosher salt
1 tablespoon white truffle oil

MAKE THE DOUGH In the bowl of a stand mixer fitted with the dough hook attachment, combine the flour and yeast and mix on low speed. With the mixer running, stream in the olive oil. Add the lukewarm water and mix until combined. Continue to knead the dough in the mixer for 5 minutes, or until smooth. Alternatively, mix the dough by hand, stirring with a wooden spoon while streaming in the oil. Turn the dough out onto a well-floured surface and knead until smooth. With about 1 minute to go, whether using the mixer or making it by hand, knead in the salt.

*I like King Arthur's flour.

continued

Divide the dough evenly in half and form it into two balls. Dust a rimmed baking sheet with flour. Place the dough on the baking sheet and cover with a kitchen towel or loosely with plastic wrap. Let the dough sit at room temperature until it has doubled in size, about 1 hour. At this point, the dough can be wrapped in plastic (if not already) and reserved in the refrigerator until ready to use, up to 3 days.

MAKE THE FILLING In the bowl of a stand mixer fitted with the whisk attachment or in a mixing bowl, combine the ricotta and herbs. Set aside.

In a small glass bowl, microwave the Taleggio on low power until melted, about 2 minutes, stopping and stirring it every 15 to 20 seconds. Alternatively, you can melt the cheese in a double boiler (a small metal or glass bowl placed over a small simmering pot of water). You just want to avoid letting the cheese come into direct contact with the heat or the cheese will get weird.

When the Taleggio is melty, immediately stir it into the ricotta. The Taleggio should be smooth and the ricotta whipped a bit when you are done. The filling can be made ahead and refrigerated for up to 5 days; let it sit at room temperature for about 1 hour before serving, so it's easier to spread.

BAKE THE FOCACCIA Preheat the oven to 500°F with a pizza stone or rimless baking sheet on the lowest rack. You want your oven to preheat for at least 30 minutes so that everything is good and hot.

On a well-floured surface, roll one half of the dough into a roughly round shape that's ¼ inch thick. Carefully transfer the dough to a pizza peel or another rimless baking sheet (see page 150).

Using a fork, poke as many holes as you can in the surface of the dough (docking). This prevents the dough from puffing up when it hits the hot oven. Brush half of the olive oil over the entire surface of the focaccia and sprinkle with ½ teaspoon of the salt. Carefully slide the dough onto the pizza stone or baking sheet and bake for 5 minutes, or until the focaccia just starts to brown. Keep an eye on it. If the dough starts to puff, just beat it down with a fork. A few bubbles are okay, but make sure it doesn't go full pita on you. Roll, dock, and oil the remaining dough. When the first focaccia is done, slide the second into the oven.

SLICE, STUFF, AND SERVE Here's the trickiest thing in the book: Have a bread knife ready when you remove the focaccia from the oven. As soon as it's out, insert the tip of your knife into the side of the focaccia and slide the blade to the center to cut it in half through its very thin equator. A kitchen towel is handy here for rotating the focaccia as you slice it. With a little practice, or beginner's luck, you can do this. Work quickly! (If you mess it up, just cut the dough into 8 pizza slices, dip them into the ricotta mix, and drizzle with the truffle oil.) At this point, you should have a top and bottom for each focaccia.

Using a cake-icing spatula or any other spatula, spread the ricotta mix over the bottom of the focaccia. Drizzle with the truffle oil and season with the remaining ¼ teaspoon salt.

Replace the top half of each focaccia, pressing a bit so the oil pushes through the holes in the top. Return it to the oven for an additional 2 minutes, or until golden brown and a bit bubbly.

Slice each focaccia into 8 pieces and serve hot, salty, and melty.

PITA OUT OF PIZZA DOUGH!

MAKES 8 PITAS

Basically, if you take our pizza dough, divide it into eight balls instead of two, roll it instead of stretching it, and then let it puff up on your pizza stone, it's pretty delicious pita. End of story. It's a thousand times better than what you can find at the store, which honestly is more like cardboard than bread. Even the stuff you get from the pita bakery is only so-so. This is hands-down the easiest and best way to get great pita at home, and people get pretty excited when they see them all puffed, fresh out of the oven. And you can use 'em for everything: obviously to wipe up your hummus, to make great sandwiches, to use in place of crepes for Frenchy-Style Fish Tacos (see page 198), to schmear some spread inside and stuff with leftover fish or chicken, to top with some grain salad. I mean, anything in this book is fair game for going on, in, or around a pita. And then with day-old pitas, you can split 'em, toast 'em, and use 'em in place of bread for panzanellas.

A couple things to note: If you want the pitas to puff up and get a little crispier—like if you're going to use them for dipping or scooping—don't oil them first. But if you're going to use them for a sandwich, go ahead and brush one side with oil before baking them, which will help them stay a little more pliable. Also, when your pita puffs up, don't just grab it with your hand. They're like little steam engines inside and they'll burn you real bad. Tongs are your friend here.

1 recipe Pizza Dough (page 150),
    divided into 8 balls
Extra-virgin olive oil (optional)

GET YOUR OVEN HOT Preheat the oven to 500°F with a pizza stone or rimless baking sheet on the lowest rack. Let your oven heat for at least 30 minutes before you cook the pitas.

ROLL AND BAKE On a well-floured surface, roll each dough ball into an 8-inch circle that's ⅛ to ¼ inch thick (or something close-ish; don't sweat it). Working in batches of two, pick up each circle of dough and knock off any extra flour. If you're going for a nice, puffed, slightly crisp pita, place the dough on your pizza stone and bake until puffed, about 3 minutes. Use a pancake turner or tongs to flip the pitas over and bake the other side until golden, about 3 minutes longer. Transfer the pitas to a kitchen towel–lined basket or bowl while you continue to bake the rest of the pitas. If you want a slightly chewier pita for making sandwiches, lightly oil one side of the dough before baking. Place the dough on the stone oil-side up and bake without flipping it, about 6 minutes.

SERVE OR STORE Serve warm! Store leftover, fully cooled pita in an airtight container at room temperature for up to 2 days. To reheat, wrap tightly in foil and warm in a 250°F oven.

2

This chapter is pretty much based on the original avec prosciutto plate, where we serve it thinly sliced alongside other ingredients like beautiful raw white asparagus and hazelnut vinaigrette or cherries or kohlrabi or stone fruit and hard cheese. The basic idea is that we wanted to showcase really good cured meat—usually La Quercia from Herb Eckhouse—alongside something fresh, like a meat salad that you eat with your hands. It's also an upgrade from the too-common giant pile of meat on a serving plate, as if it's sort of an afterthought. I generally like cured meats thinly sliced, except for sausages, which you can cut into small chunks, and summer sausages and, occasionally, salami, which can be good cut into cubes. It's delicious, and it's certainly great on a crusty loaf that you schmear some butter on, but this is just a little more thoughtful of an approach than meat-on-meat-on-meat. And it isn't really a technique so much as an idea.

When I first sat down to write these recipes, I tried to be specific about which meats would go nicely with what, but it's all about not being specific. Spicy Italian sausage? Delicious. Coppa? Sure! Country ham? No problem. Salami, merguez, prosciutto, summer sausage, grilled fresh sausage—it all works. And these days you can find great cured meats and sausages everywhere (except in the Wisconsin North Woods, in which case your only options are beef jerky and summer sausage—no complaints). Put together one or two of these recipes and serve them as a starter or for people to get into while you're standing around and cooking, or as a side dish to chicken or fish. Possibilities? Limitless.

ADD SOME CURED MEATS AND GRILLED SAUSAGE

To Drink

Beer. Definitely beer. Go with something a little hoppier, like a lighter IPA. Or go for a red wine with some acidity and a slight chill on it—Grenache, Gamay, a red Txakolina. If you prefer whites try, a dry (Michigan) Riesling or Grüner Veltliner. And there's always rosé.

SALUMI OR SAUSAGE WITH PICKLED CHERRIES, FENNEL, AND HARD CHEESE

These are all things that are awesome with cured meats on their own—a bowl of cherries, a plate of shaved fennel, a good hard cheese. Here you're just putting 'em together.

Pickled Cherries

1 cup red wine vinegar
¼ cup sugar
5 sprigs thyme
1 dried árbol chile, or ¼ teaspoon crushed red chile flakes
1 teaspoon kosher salt
1 pound fresh sweet cherries, stemmed, pitted, and halved*

1 small bulb fennel, sliced as thinly as you can (use a mandoline if you have one)
¼ cup reserved fennel tops, coarsely chopped
¼ cup Italian parsley leaves
2 tablespoons extra-virgin olive oil
½ teaspoon kosher salt
6 cranks black pepper
6 to 8 ounces cured meat or grilled sausage
2 ounces hard cheese, such as Parmigiano or aged Gruyère, thinly sliced with a vegetable peeler

54

MAKE THE PICKLED CHERRIES In a medium pot, combine all of the ingredients except the cherries. Bring to a simmer over medium heat and simmer until the sugar dissolves, about 2 minutes. Decrease the heat to low and add the cherries. Cook for 1 minute, then remove the pot from the heat. Let the cherries cool to room temperature. Once cooled, the cherries will keep in an airtight container in the fridge for about 1 month. (Any leftovers can be used in another salad, with roasted pork or chicken, or served with a cheese board or charcuterie.)

PUT IT TOGETHER AND SERVE In a large bowl, combine 1 cup of the pickled cherries and 1 tablespoon of the pickling liquid with the fennel bulb and fronds, the parsley, oil, salt, and pepper. Toss together. Arrange the meat on a serving plate. Heap the cherry mixture on top of the meat. Sprinkle the cheese over the top and serve.

*Tart cherries would be good, too.

ADD SOME CURED MEATS AND GRILLED SAUSAGE

SALUMI OR GRILLED SAUSAGE WITH WHIPPED FETA AND CRUSHED CUCUMBERS

MAKES 6 SERVINGS

The whipped feta takes something that can otherwise be pretty mundane and angular in flavor and turns it into something really delicious, and with minimal effort. And the crushed cucumbers—especially if you get the little Kirbys, which are incredible as a stand-alone and should become part of your simple cooking repertoire either way—are high in acidity with some good heat from the crushed chile flakes. The combination of the two blows my mind, it's so easy and special and definitely calls for some sausage.

Whipped Feta

6 ounces feta or goat cheese
2 tablespoons cream cheese
¼ cup heavy cream
¼ cup plain Greek yogurt
2 tablespoons extra-virgin olive oil

Crushed Cucumbers

1 pound Persian, English, or
    Kirby cucumbers
3 tablespoons sugar
2 teaspoons kosher salt

2 tablespoons freshly squeezed
    lemon juice
2 tablespoons extra-virgin olive oil
½ teaspoon crushed red chile flakes

6 to 8 ounces cured meats or grilled
    sausage of choice, cut into chunks
½ cup mint leaves, torn
¼ cup dill leaves, coarsely chopped
1 small red onion, sliced as thinly as
    you can
2 tablespoons extra-virgin olive oil

MAKE THE WHIPPED FETA Combine the feta or goat cheese, cream cheese, cream, yogurt, and oil in the bowl of a food processor. Process until well combined and smooth. Set aside until ready to use, or store in the fridge for up to 5 days.

MAKE THE CRUSHED CUCUMBERS On a cutting board, smash (the shit out of) your cucumbers with a rolling pin. I suggest covering them with plastic wrap so the guts don't fly everywhere. You should have irregularly shaped chunks of cucumber and seeds. If there are a lot of seeds, discard them. Cut the remaining hunks of cucumber into bite-size pieces. Toss them into a large bowl with the sugar and salt and let them sit for 30 minutes.

Drain the excess liquid from the bowl. Add the lemon juice, oil, and chile flakes and stir to combine. The dressed cucumbers will keep in the refrigerator for a couple of days before they break down and get a little too soggy.

SERVE Schmear the whipped feta on a serving plate. Spread the cured meats or sausages over the feta. Scatter the cucumbers, mint, dill, and onion over the meat and drizzle with the oil.

SALUMI OR GRILLED SAUSAGE WITH SUMMER SQUASH, CARROTS, AND GREEN SAUCE #2

MAKES 6 SERVINGS

Green Sauce #2 elevates summer squash and carrots, which are two vegetables that will always benefit from a little fat.

Green Sauce #2

1 cup plain Greek yogurt
½ cup extra-virgin olive oil
½ cup Italian parsley leaves
½ cup cilantro leaves
¼ cup freshly squeezed lemon juice
1 small jalapeño chile, stem removed but not seeded
2 tablespoons ground cumin
1 tablespoon ground coriander
1 clove garlic, peeled
1 teaspoon kosher salt

8 ounces summer squash (zucchini or yellow squash), sliced as thinly as you can*
8 ounces carrots, peeled and thinly shaved using a vegetable peeler or mandoline
6 to 8 ounces cured meats or grilled sausage of choice, cut into chunks
¼ cup chopped dill leaves
1 tablespoon extra-virgin olive oil

MAKE THE GREEN SAUCE Combine the yogurt, oil, parsley, cilantro, lemon juice, jalapeño, cumin, coriander, garlic, and salt in a blender and blend on high speed until smooth. Set aside or store in the fridge for up to 5 days.

DRESS AND SERVE In a large bowl, combine the squash, carrots, and ½ cup of the green sauce. Toss and let the mixture sit for a couple of minutes, until the squash softens slightly. Arrange the cured meats on a serving plate and scatter the salad around it. Spoon on some of the sauce, then top with the dill and oil.

*Use a mandoline, if you have one, or a veggie peeler.

ADD SOME CURED MEATS AND GRILLED SAUSAGE

SALUMI OR GRILLED SAUSAGE WITH WATERMELON, TOMATO, AND FETA

This dish in particular screams "grilled encased meats!" to me, and summer—obviously. Tomatoes, watermelon, and feta are the essence of late summer and are really great with any sausage you can toss on the grill.

2 cups cubed watermelon
    (½-inch cubes)
2 cups cherry tomatoes, halved
1 small red onion, sliced as thinly as
    you can
½ cup mint leaves, torn
½ cup basil leaves, torn

¼ cup extra-virgin olive oil
2 tablespoons red wine vinegar
1 teaspoon kosher salt
6 to 8 ounces cured meat or grilled
    sausage of choice, cut into chunks
4 ounces feta cheese

MAKE THE SALAD In a large bowl, combine the watermelon, cherry tomatoes, onion, mint, basil, oil, vinegar, and salt. Toss until well coated.

PUT IT TOGETHER AND SERVE Place the cured meats or sausages on a serving plate. Scatter the watermelon salad over the meat, crumble the cheese over the top, and serve.

61

SALUMI OR GRILLED SAUSAGE WITH ORANGES, DATES, AND GREEN OLIVES

Not much to do here; just combine brown sugar-y sweet dates with brininess and a little acidity from green olives and oranges, and the dish really sings.

2 navel oranges, peeled and cut into bite-size pieces

1 cup fresh Medjool dates, pitted and quartered

1 small red onion, sliced as thinly as you can

½ cup pitted Castelvetrano or other green olives, such as Lucques or Picholine, halved

½ cup Italian parsley leaves

2 tablespoons extra-virgin olive oil

1 tablespoon freshly squeezed lemon juice

½ teaspoon kosher salt

¼ teaspoon crushed red chile flakes

6 to 8 ounces cured meat or grilled sausage of choice, cut into chunks

MIX THE TOPPING Combine the oranges, dates, onion, olives, parsley, oil, lemon juice, salt, and chile flakes in a large bowl. Give the mixture a few good tosses, until it's well mixed.

PUT IT TOGETHER AND SERVE Place the cured meats or sausages on a serving plate. Scatter the orange mixture over the meat and serve.

3

Tossing a salad together seems mindless, but making a good one really requires some thoughtfulness. In restaurants, the first job you have is making salads. It's a way to teach you about the balance between the fresh greens and the fat, acidity, and salt of the dressing. A great salad doesn't have to be tons of complicated ingredients; it can be as simple as really good arugula with great olive oil, salt, and black pepper. A formula we use in the restaurant and I replicate at home is greens, a fruit, a nut, and a bit of cheese with a great vinaigrette. Sometimes I'll throw a surprise herb, such as basil, tarragon, chervil, or chives, in there because it sort of wakes up the greens a little bit. And then there's the greens themselves. In general, I like to mix a more neutral-tasting lettuce that's one of the more sweet and juicy varieties (Little Gem, kale, romaine, etc.) with a more bitter one (frisée, escarole, endive, etc.). Any combination will work, and all of the recipes in this chapter will work with all of the greens.

BUY SOME GREENS

To Drink

You want minerality and high acidity, like a Spanish Albariño or Greek Assyrtiko.

Anything bright, fresh, and green (basil, mint, cucumber) will be great with Sauvignon Blanc, ideally French. (And rosé.)

here's
how

TOSS TOGETHER SOME GREENS (AND HERBS)

Be smart about what greens you choose, and choose good ones. A salad can only be as good as its greens—or any of its ingredients, really—so it's worth the extra effort to go to the farmers' market or a good grocery store and find a nice, lively head of lettuce. It's the difference between an okay-ish salad and one that's downright ethereal.

As for how you prepare your salad, in general I prefer a leaf that's 3 to 4 inches long in terms of bite-size eatability. Or if you're someone who likes salads full of little bits, that's fine, too. I personally prefer a salad that you could pretty much eat with your hands, which in my house is not out of the question.

Tossing herbs into a salad helps bridge flavors (think mozzarella to tomato), adds flavor to more one-dimensional ingredients (lemon, olive oil, butter lettuce + tarragon is delicious, simple, and eye-opening), and contributes a bright, cleansing point to heartier dishes. If you do add herbs—and I highly recommend you do—don't mince them up. It's not something you want the whole salad to taste like; you just want little pops of flavor. Just tear the leaves if it's a larger variety (chervil, basil) or add whole leaves for smaller ones (tarragon). The best way to do it is to snip the leaves with scissors, coarsely run a knife through them, or just use your hands to tear.

Here's a guide to greens, listed by category and in order of my personal preference, from most to least favorite. I recommend picking one from categories for each of these recipes, plus an herb. Then give your lettuces a quick wash in cool water and drain well in a salad spinner so any remaining water doesn't dilute the dressing.

Neutral Greens

LITTLE GEM: This is technically a variety of romaine and is a tight little head that's super-crisp and juicy. Cut the core out, tear off the leaves, and that's it. Like romaine, the farther you get from the white core toward the darker green ends, the less texture there is in the leaf. The dark green leaves can be a little flabby, so I discard them.

BABY HEADS OF LETTUCE (OR "TEENAGE" LETTUCE): This includes lettuces like red oak, green oak, or the hundreds of different seed varieties that farmers grow of smaller heads of lettuce. We're not talking about iceberg; we're looking for lettuces that are bright and fresh. If the outside leaves are a little brown, just peel them off. Then, to separate the leaves, peel them away until you get to the core. Leave them as-is if they're on the smaller side or whack them into halves or quarters.

KALE (ALL VARIETIES—TUSCAN, DINOSAUR, LACINATO, CURLY, ETC.): For a lot of green salads, you just give them a quick toss right before you're ready to eat, but kale takes a bit more prep. You need to take out the hearty ribs, tear the leaves, and give them a little massage, which you can do an hour or more in advance. Kale can go from being super-sweet and tender in the fall when it gets cold to pretty woody and leathery in the summer, so use that as a gauge to decide how much you need to break down the leaves. You just want to work them with your hands until they're tender. Don't be afraid to get in there—it's kale. It's not a gentle massage; it's a full deep-tissue treatment. You can skip this if you're using baby kale. After the massage, coarsely cut the leaves into smaller ribbons or pieces.

68

COOKING FOR GOOD TIMES

SPINACH: You've got your baby spinach and then the heartier spinach—both will work. One key thing either way is that because it's so tender and prone to getting wilty, you don't want to dress it too early—add it last to a salad and dress it gently. And don't go 100 percent spinach.

HEARTY HEADS OF RED- AND GREEN-LEAF LETTUCE: The key here is "hearty." If the leaves are all floppy, too tender, or bruised or battered, that's no good. Look for a nice, tight head of lettuce and always remove the more-mature outer leaves. Work with the inner three-quarters of the head. This is more of a tearing lettuce than a cutting lettuce.

BIBB: Like spinach, this is super-tender and tends to turn to mush on the plate. You want to be careful not to dress it too heavily or work it too much. Dress it right before you're going to serve it, preferably with a lighter vinaigrette.

ROMAINE HEARTS: This is everywhere; you could buy it at a gas station. Get rid of the darker green leaves, just chop up the larger outer leaves, and leave the smaller leaves whole once you get to the middle of the head. These in particular become great little cups for dressing, cheese, and all-around great flavors to hang out in.

Bitter Greens

ARUGULA: We're not necessarily talking about the stuff in the clamshell, which has a really mild, kind of tepid flavor. The arugula you most often find in the grocery store is a sort of mutated version of wild arugula and, to me, tastes kind of anemic. It's okay, but I prefer the traditional round-leaf variety called "rocket." You usually see it in big bunches, but sometimes it's sold in a clamshell, and it has a hotter, spicier flavor. That heat is similar to acidity, so if it's balanced with other greens, it's really good.

FRISÉE: Like all the chicories, frisée is bitter and a little sweet at the same time, which is great. For me, frisée plus arugula plus a neutral lettuce is a super combo. All you have to do is trim off the outer leaves, and just like with romaine, trim off the top ¾ to 1 inch of the darker leaves so you're dealing mostly with the yellow.

RADICCHIO (OR ANY OTHER ITALIAN CHICORIES, SUCH AS TREVISO, TARDIVO, CASTELFRANCO, ESCAROLE, AND LOTS OF OTHER VARIETIES): I personally love how super-bitter these are, but it's not for everyone. So you just need to add something sweeter to balance it, like Little Gem. Cut the core out and tear 'em up.

BELGIAN ENDIVE: This isn't quite as bitter as the others—it's like a great gateway drug to the other bitter greens. It's very hearty, too, almost like a Little Gem, so you can build a salad on it and it can sit through the whole dinner without turning to mush. Counter to what I said earlier, I actually like any of these salads with just endive. It works with just about anything, and I like separating the leaves instead of slicing them so they're nice little scoops.

CURLY ENDIVE: This is like the grandfather to frisée. It has a lime green heart that basically tastes the same as frisée, and when you find a head that's three-quarters that color, then it's really amazing. So if you open up a head and see that there's a decent amount of that lime green, you should buy it because it will be delicious. I would make a salad with just curly endive any day of the week, but I'm a bitter freak.

Herbs

TARRAGON: This herb is licorice-like, earthy, funky, and adds layers of flavor to simple ingredients. It's great with lettuces, and especially tasty with chicken.

BASIL: Strong, earthy, bright, basil plays well with most fruit—don't forget tomato is a fruit!

CHERVIL: This one has a subtle anise flavor. It's best with mild-tasting ingredients like butter lettuce when just a little flavor makes a difference.

CHIVES: These are bright, spicy onions that are good with stronger flavors when you want onion, but not the strength of diced onion or the lingering breath.

MINT: Always refreshing and bright, use mint with earthy flavors to bring them alive.

PARSLEY: With its clean, grassy flavor, parsley is a general workhorse that cleanses and bridges flavors more than it adds flavor.

GREENS WITH TZATZIKI VINAIGRETTE, POTATOES, AND GREEN BEANS

MAKES 6 SERVINGS

This is a play on the Greek sauce, but thinned out a bit to work as a vinaigrette with a bunch of dill added. Then I toss in cooked potatoes, green beans, and cucumber.

Tzatziki Vinaigrette
½ cup extra-virgin olive oil
½ small shallot
¼ cup plain Greek yogurt
¼ cup dill leaves, chopped
2 tablespoons freshly squeezed
    lemon juice
1 clove garlic, peeled
½ teaspoon kosher salt
6 cranks black pepper

2 tablespoons plus ¼ teaspoon
    kosher salt
1 cup green beans, stems removed,
    cut into 1-inch pieces
4 small red potatoes, cut into ⅛-inch
    slices
1 small cucumber, thinly sliced*
½ cup pitted black olives, such as
    Kalamata
4 cups trimmed and washed greens
    (see page 68)

MAKE THE VINAIGRETTE Combine the oil, shallot, yogurt, dill, lemon juice, garlic, salt, and pepper in a blender and let it rip. Blend until the vinaigrette is completely smooth. Set aside until ready to use or store in the fridge for up to 5 days.

COOK THE BEANS In a large saucepan, bring 4 cups of water to a boil over high heat. Add 2 tablespoons of the salt and the green beans. Cook for 2 minutes, or until bright green and tender but still crisp. Remove the beans from the water and immediately stash them in the fridge while you finish cooking the other ingredients.

COOK THE POTATOES Return the water to a boil and add the potatoes. Cook for 7 minutes, or until fork-tender but not so soft that they're falling apart. Strain and place in the fridge to cool completely.

PUT IT TOGETHER AND SERVE In a large bowl, combine the cold green beans and potatoes with the cucumber, olives, and greens. Evenly coat the greens with the vinaigrette and taste the salad. Add more vinaigrette to your liking, or serve the remaining vinaigrette on the side.

71

*I prefer the Persian ones.

GREENS WITH ROASTED SHALLOT VINAIGRETTE, FRUIT, NUTS, AND YUMMY CHEESE

MAKES 6 SERVINGS

We usually have some variation of this on the avec menu. For me, the star is the vinaigrette, which is peeled, halved, and roasted shallots as opposed to the classic raw shallot. So you're tempering that onion-yness and getting a sweeter, richer flavor. The great news is that after you've roasted the shallots, everything just gets dumped in the blender. Done.

Roasted Shallot Vinaigrette

2 small shallots
½ cup plus 1 tablespoon extra-virgin olive oil
½ teaspoon kosher salt
¼ cup red wine vinegar
1 teaspoon honey
½ teaspoon Dijon mustard
6 cranks black pepper

4 cups trimmed and washed greens (see page 68)
1 cup fruit, such as blackberries, strawberries, sliced pear, or sliced apple
2 tablespoons tarragon leaves
Pinch of salt
6 cranks black pepper
½ cup roasted, salted nuts, such as Marcona almonds, hazelnuts, or walnuts
2 ounces yummy hard cheese, such as Parmigiano, Pecorino, or anything else you can use a peeler on

MAKE THE VINAIGRETTE Preheat the oven to 350°F. On a small rimmed baking sheet, combine the shallots, 1 tablespoon of the oil, and ¼ teaspoon of the salt. Toss well, then roast until tender and starting to brown, about 15 minutes. Add the roasted shallots, vinegar, honey, mustard, pepper, and the remaining ¼ teaspoon salt to a blender and let it run on high speed until smooth. While running, slowly drizzle in the remaining ½ cup oil through the hole in the lid. Set aside until ready to use or store in the fridge in a tightly sealed container for up to 5 days.

PUT IT TOGETHER AND SERVE In a large bowl, combine the greens, fruit, and tarragon. Add half of the vinaigrette plus the salt and pepper. Toss thoroughly (use your hands and get in there, but be gentle). Give the salad a taste and add more vinaigrette if it seems dry. Top the salad with the nuts. Using a peeler, shave the cheese over the salad. Serve the remaining vinaigrette on the side.

GREENS WITH LEMON-YOGURT VINAIGRETTE, RADISHES, MINT, AND SEED CRACKERS

MAKES 6 SERVINGS

This recipe is a great way to use leftover Seed Crackers, which are like a crouton here. Bonus points for finding a Meyer lemon for the vinaigrette. If you use a standard lemon, add the honey to give it some sweetness.

Lemon-Yogurt Vinaigrette
½ cup extra-virgin olive oil
¼ cup plain Greek yogurt
¼ cup freshly squeezed Meyer or
  Eureka lemon juice
2 teaspoons honey (optional; add
  if using a Eureka lemon)
1 small clove garlic, grated on a
  rasp grater
½ teaspoon kosher salt, plus more
  as needed
¼ teaspoon crushed red chile flakes

4 cups trimmed and washed greens
  (see page 68)
1 cup paper-thin sliced radishes
  (about 8 large radishes)
1 cup Seed Crackers (page 40) or
  other good whole-grain seed-y
  crackers, broken into 1- to 2-inch
  shards
1 small bunch mint, leaves removed
Pinch of kosher salt
6 cranks black pepper

MAKE THE VINAIGRETTE Combine the oil, yogurt, lemon juice, garlic, salt, and chile flakes in a small jar with a tight-fitting lid. Shake! Taste it, add more salt if necessary, and shake it again. Set aside until ready to use or store in the fridge for up to 5 days.

PUT IT TOGETHER AND SERVE In a large bowl, combine the greens, radishes, crackers, mint, salt, and pepper. Toss with half of the vinaigrette and give it a taste. Add more vinaigrette if the salad seems dry or serve the rest of the vinaigrette on the side.

CHARRED RADICCHIO WITH ARUGULA, CHERRIES, AND PARMIGIANO

MAKES 6 SERVINGS

This is a technique that I've used for chicories for a long time because they're bitter but have a lot of locked-in sugar content that comes out when you take them pretty far over ripping-hot heat. Then when you smoodge 'em with lemon juice and balsamic or saba—and, of course, salt and pepper—it creates a whole new level of depth of flavor that's true to life factual big time. Period.

2 small heads radicchio, cut into
    1-inch slices
3 tablespoons balsamic vinegar,
    plus more as needed*
1½ teaspoons kosher salt, plus
    more as needed
6 cranks black pepper

¼ cup plus 2 tablespoons extra-virgin
    olive oil
2 tablespoons freshly squeezed
    lemon juice, plus more as needed
1 cup fresh cherries, pitted**
3 cups hearty arugula
2 ounces Parmigiano cheese

CHAR THE RADICCHIO In a large bowl, toss the radicchio with 2 tablespoons of the vinegar, 1 teaspoon of the salt, and half of the pepper. Let the mixture marinate while you heat a large heavy-bottomed sauté pan over high heat. Add 2 tablespoons of the oil.

When the oil looks very hot (almost smoking), carefully add the radicchio to the pan so it sits in one layer. You may need to do this in batches. Cook on one side until charred and just starting to soften, 2 to 4 minutes. Transfer to a large bowl.

PUT IT TOGETHER AND SERVE Add the remaining 1 tablespoon vinegar and 1 tablespoon of the lemon juice to the bowl. Toss and taste. It'll be pretty bitter, but feel free to add more salt, lemon juice, or vinegar. Let the radicchio cool to room temperature.

Add the remaining ¼ cup oil, 1 tablespoon lemon juice, ½ teaspoon salt, and pepper plus the cherries to the bowl and give everything a good toss. Add the arugula and give it one more good toss. Using a peeler or rasp grater, peel or grate the cheese over the top of the salad and serve.

*Bonus points for good balsamic, or saba if you can find it.
**This also would be good with sliced pear, apple, or peach.

CHARRED KALE WITH BEEFSTEAK TOMATOES AND PINE NUTS

We've all eaten a ton of marinated kale, but when you throw it into a smoking-hot pan, it creates a whole 'nother level of tastiness that's totally unexpected.

Marinated Kale

¼ cup grated Pecorino or Parmigiano cheese
2 tablespoons extra-virgin olive oil
Zest and juice of 1 lemon
1 clove garlic, minced
½ teaspoon honey
½ teaspoon kosher salt
¼ teaspoon crushed red chile flakes
Freshly ground black pepper

1 large bunch black Tuscan kale, thick ribs removed and leaves torn into big pieces

3 large beefsteak tomatoes, cut into ¼-inch slices
2 tablespoons extra-virgin olive oil
½ teaspoon flaky salt*
¼ cup pine nuts, toasted in a skillet until aromatic

MARINATE THE KALE In a large bowl, combine the cheese, oil, lemon zest and juice, garlic, honey, salt, chile flakes, and a couple grinds of pepper. Add the kale and toss to combine. Really get in there and work the kale (go rough massage), then let the kale marinate at room temperature for 2 hours or in the refrigerator overnight.

CHAR THE KALE Preheat a large cast-iron pan over high heat for 5 minutes. When the pan looks very hot (like little wisps of smoke), add the marinated kale and char on one side for 1 minute. You are just looking for char and to heat the kale, not to fully cook it. This could also be done over the high heat of a grill. Remove from the heat.

PUT IT TOGETHER AND SERVE Lay the tomatoes on a platter, drizzle with the oil, sprinkle with the salt, top with the charred kale and pine nuts, and serve.

79

Charring Greens

Charring greens, or throwing them on a super-hot grill or pan, is a great way to get nice smoky flavor into your salad—or anything else, really. You're not cooking the greens, just starting to caramelize some of the sugars while leaving some of the head raw. In the lettuce category, I'd go with kale, Little Gem, or romaine. For bitter greens, I'd choose frisée, radicchio (or other chicories), or endive. Just split or quarter the head depending on size, brush with a little oil (don't use much—you don't want the grill to flare up and make the lettuce taste like gasoline), season with salt and pepper, and sear it hard for about 1 minute. Don't flip it. Then toss it in whichever vinaigrette you're going to use.

*Go for the good stuff here, such as Maldon.

4

Beets have pretty much always been on the menu at avec, mostly because they're accessible year-round, and delicious. In the spring, you're just pulling 'em from the ground, and they're on the smaller side; earthy and sweet. Then by fall, they're ready for cold storage to get you through the winter, and that's when you see the softball-size guys that don't really have the same sugary quality that their younger counterparts do. Enter our classic beet-roasting method, which has been part of my personal rotation for years because it rounds out the natural bitter flavor of beets. We've modified it a bit so it also suits sweet potatoes and turnips—both excellent, versatile roots. First we roast the vegetables to concentrate their sweetness, and then we marinate them to bring the acidity back and balance out that sweetness. When they're warm out of the oven, they're like little sponges, soaking up all that flavor. And then you can just toss them with things like burrata and charred kale or strawberries, ricotta, and pistachios to make a really substantial, balanced dish.

A lot of the big techniques in this book are pretty protein-forward, but that's not necessarily the way I cook all the time. When you're working your way through a dinner, you want more vegetables and vegetable-based mains on the table, not just a piece of meat. This method is going to give you the kinds of dishes to get you there.

ROAST SOME ROOTS

To Drink

Go for Chardonnays that are low in the oak department (that is, White Burgundy / Chablis). Pinot Noir and lighter rustic reds like Grenache, young Bandol, or Corsican Nielluccio would be great with these recipes, as would some of the Spanish natural ("natty") reds that are low in alcohol and a little on the funky side. Or a slightly sweeter brown ale. (Or rosé.)

here's how

PREP, ROAST, AND MARINATE ROOT VEGETABLES

This technique is perfect when you're cooking for friends and family because it takes way less time than roasting the vegetables whole—thirty to forty minutes tops—and they can be roasted ahead, which just means they spend more time hanging out in their tasty marinade in the fridge. Then they're ready to be tossed back in the pan to be crisped up again—or not. They're delicious at room temperature, or even served cold. It's the kind of thing you want to have in your back pocket.

MAKES 6 SERVINGS

2 pounds beets, sweet potatoes, or turnips
   (any color, golf ball- to baseball-size)
¼ cup rice bran oil, grapeseed oil, or olive oil*
1 tablespoon kosher salt
2 teaspoons sugar or honey
1 teaspoon freshly ground black pepper
2 sprigs thyme
2 sprigs rosemary
Juice of 1 orange or lemon, or 2 tablespoons
   red, champagne, or cider vinegar
2 tablespoons extra-virgin olive oil
½ teaspoon crushed red chile flakes

Prep

Preheat the oven to 350°F.

Depending on the size and type of the root, peel it or not. Peel the dirty, gnarly beets. Sweet potato skins soften up when roasting, so leave those on. For thinner-skinned turnips, a good scrubbing will do.

Cut the roots into chunks; I like them about 1 inch thick and 2 inches long. Cut the round roots through the equator and chunk them up from there. For sweet potatoes, cut them in half lengthwise, then again lengthwise, and then into 2-inch pieces. If you can find baby sweet potatoes, just cut those in half. There's no wrong way to do this; just keep all of your vegetables similar in size and shape so they cook evenly.

Roast

Preheat an ovenproof sauté pan large enough to hold the root vegetables in one layer over medium-high heat. Add the rice bran, grapeseed, or olive oil and continue heating until the oil shimmers and is thinking about smoking. Carefully add the roots and let them caramelize on one side, 2 to 3 minutes. Check to make sure they're not burning—lower the heat if they're scorching in some spots. Give the roots a toss in the pan (tongs work, too) and season with the salt, sugar, and pepper. Add the thyme and rosemary and transfer the pan to the oven.

Cook until the vegetables are lightly browned and tender. Start checking with the tip of a sharp knife after 6 minutes and continue to check every 5 minutes. They're done when they're easily pierced all the way through. The beets will cook in about 30 minutes, the turnips in 10 minutes or less, and the sweet potatoes in 20 minutes. This will depend on the age, variety, and cut of the vegetable, so use your senses (including common sense) and check often.

Marinate

Spoon the roasted vegetables into a large bowl. Discard the herb stems. Add the orange juice or vinegar, extra-virgin olive oil, and chile flakes. Toss until well coated.

Serve

You can serve at this point, or store in the fridge for up to 5 days.

*Save the extra-virgin for something else.

ROASTED AND MARINATED BEETS WITH BURRATA, CHARRED KALE, AND HAZELNUT VINAIGRETTE

MAKES 6 SERVINGS

This is a really, really exceptional dish that always blows people's minds. It speaks exactly to that incredible thing that happens after you've marinated root vegetables and then charred them, and this time we're adding some Tuscan kale to the marinade and charring it in the cast-iron skillet along with the roots. Then, because I'm a nut-vinaigrette freak, everything gets tossed in a hazelnut vinaigrette. Nut oils have that same combination of earthy and sweet as root vegetables, which makes them the dream team, and then the oil has all that extra fat and richness that's just delicious. I top this off with burrata, which might seem like a cop-out because adding burrata to things is like adding caviar—it's cheating a little bit—but the creaminess against the roasted veg is just out of this world. And it doesn't necessarily need the ooze factor, so you could use fresh mozzarella instead. Could you just add the cheese to the roasted roots along with some marinated kale? Yeah. Would it be unique? Yeah. But the whole extra step of searing the beets and kale and pouring them right from the pan onto a platter? Next level.

If you've already roasted and marinated the beets, you could marinate the kale on its own, then sear everything together.

Marinated Kale

¼ cup grated Pecorino or
    Parmigiano cheese
2 tablespoons extra-virgin olive oil
Zest and juice of 1 lemon
1 clove garlic, minced
½ teaspoon honey
½ teaspoon kosher salt
¼ teaspoon crushed red chile flakes
Freshly ground black pepper
1 large bunch black Tuscan kale, ribs
    remove, coarsely chopped

Hazelnut Vinaigrette

Heaping ¼ cup hazelnuts, toasted in
    a skillet over medium heat until
    fragrant and then finely ground
3 tablespoons hazelnut oil
1 tablespoon red wine vinegar
1 teaspoon finely chopped shallot
1 teaspoon minced thyme leaves
½ teaspoon honey
¼ teaspoon kosher salt
3 cranks black pepper

Roasted and marinated beets
    (see page 84)
2 balls burrata or fresh mozzarella
    cheese, torn into rough chunks
Kosher salt
Freshly ground black pepper
½ cup coarsely chopped toasted
    hazelnuts

continued

ROASTED AND MARINATED BEETS WITH BURRATA, CHARRED KALE, AND HAZELNUT VINAIGRETTE

continued

MARINATE THE KALE In a large bowl, combine the cheese, olive oil, lemon zest and juice, garlic, honey, salt, chile flakes, and pepper. Add the kale and toss to combine—really get in there and work the kale with your hands; this isn't a gentle massage. Set the kale aside to marinate at room temperature for 2 hours or in the fridge overnight. Alternatively, you could toss the kale in with the just-roasted, marinating beets along with the cheese, olive oil, et al., and let the mixture sit at room temperature for 2 hours or in the fridge overnight. They'll marinate just the same.

MAKE THE VINAIGRETTE Combine the hazelnuts, hazelnut oil, vinegar, shallot, thyme, honey, salt, and pepper in a small jar with a tight-fitting lid and shake it until the dressing comes together. Set aside until ready to serve, or store in the fridge for up to 5 days.

CHAR THE KALE AND BEETS Preheat a large cast-iron pan over high heat for 5 minutes. When the pan looks very hot (you see little wisps of smoke), add the marinated beets and char on one side for 1 minute, just long enough to get some char. Remove the beets from the pan and add the kale, again charring for 1 minute. You are looking to just heat the kale, not fully cook it. You also could do this over the high heat of a grill. Remove the pan from the heat.

PUT IT TOGETHER AND SERVE Spread the cheese over a large platter. Season it a bit with salt and pepper. Scatter the charred kale and beets over the cheese, douse with the hazelnut vinaigrette, and finish with the chopped hazelnuts.

ROASTED AND MARINATED ROOTS WITH SMOKY YOGURT, CRISP LENTILS, AND DILL VINAIGRETTE

Don't let "smoky yogurt" make you think I've gone all cheffy on you. Yeah, in the restaurant the yogurt is actually smoked, but then I realized there's some great-quality smoked sea salts out there that would also give you that effect (and you have to season the yogurt with salt anyway, so there you go). Liquid smoke also came up as a way to make this recipe more home cook–friendly, and though I dismissed it as a hack at first, I don't believe the finest of palates could tell the difference between the real thing and the bottled thing. As for the crispy lentils, that idea came from Jonathon Sawyer, the amazing chef and wild man from Cleveland. He's a total process guy, and every time I talk to him he's got some technique he's doing that's really cool and delicious. He taught me that one way to get incredibly crispy lentils is to cook them until they're tender, Cryovac them with a lot of olive oil and salt, and let them cure for a month before frying them. The final product is really good, but sorry, Johnny. Perry soaks them overnight and fries them in a skillet, and they're just about as good. Perfect for all your crunchy-bit needs, or even on their own by the handful as a snack. So you got your yogurt, you got your roots, you got your chicories drizzled with dill vinaigrette, and then there's the smoky yogurt and crispy lentils over the top. It's a pretty solid deal.

89

Crisp Lentils

½ cup beluga or French lentils, soaked with water to cover by 2 inches overnight at room temperature*
¼ cup extra-virgin olive oil
½ teaspoon kosher salt
Pinch of cayenne pepper

Smoky Yogurt

1 cup plain Greek yogurt
2 tablespoons extra-virgin olive oil
1 tablespoon red wine vinegar
1 teaspoon crushed red chile flakes
1 teaspoon smoked sea salt, or a couple drops of liquid smoke, or ½ teaspoon kosher salt
1 tablespoon water

Dill Vinaigrette

¼ cup extra-virgin olive oil
1 small shallot, finely minced
2 tablespoons chopped dill leaves
Zest and juice of 1 lime
1 teaspoon brown sugar
½ teaspoon kosher salt
¼ teaspoon finely grated jalapeño chile
¼ teaspoon crushed red chile flakes

Roasted and marinated root vegetables (see page 84)
1 small head chicory, such as radicchio, Castelfranco, or endive, washed, trimmed, and separated into individual leaves
1 Fuji, Granny Smith, or other crisp apple, cored and thinly sliced
2 tablespoons chopped dill leaves

continued

*It's really important to soak the lentils; you will break your teeth trying to eat fried, unsoaked lentils. The day before you cook, soak the lentils. Soak the lentils. Soak the lentils. Don't forget to soak the lentils.

ROASTED AND MARINATED ROOTS WITH SMOKY YOGURT, CRISP LENTILS, AND DILL VINAIGRETTE

continued

MAKE THE CRISPY LENTILS Drain the lentils well, shaking off as much excess water as you can. Heat the oil in a medium sauté pan over medium high-heat until it shimmers and looks like it could almost smoke. Carefully add the lentils (they might sputter a bit) and cook until crisp, about 2 minutes, stirring often so they don't stick to the bottom. Drain off as much oil from the pan as you can and transfer the lentils to a paper towel–lined plate. Season with the kosher salt and cayenne while still warm. Set aside until ready to serve or let cool completely and store in an airtight container at room temperature for up to 5 days.

MAKE THE SMOKY YOGURT In a small bowl, combine the yogurt, oil, vinegar, chile flakes, smoked salt, and water. Whisk until well combined. Set aside until ready to serve or store in the fridge for up to 5 days.

MAKE THE DILL VINAIGRETTE Combine the oil, shallot, dill leaves, lime zest and juice, the brown sugar, kosher salt, jalapeño, and chile flakes in a small jar with a tight-fitting lid. Shake it until it all comes together. Set aside until ready to use or store in the fridge for up to 2 days (the dill gets a little funky if it sits longer than that).

PUT IT TOGETHER AND SERVE Spread the yogurt over a serving plate. Scatter the root vegetables over the yogurt and tuck in the chicory leaves and apple slices. Spoon the vinaigrette over and top with fried lentils and the chopped dill.

ROASTED AND MARINATED ROOT VEGETABLES WITH ORANGES, BLACK OLIVES, AND FETA

As a young cook, I fell in love with the combination of orange and olive—black or green. It's sort of a North African combination and it was really striking to me because they're so seemingly opposite but taste so good together. The orange is super-juicy, and then you have the salty olives—which all go really well with root vegetables, especially in the wintertime when there's not much else out there that's succulent and fresh-tasting. We also threw in some olive brine here because one of my culinary mentors, Ken Minami, taught me how to cook with it—in vinaigrettes or tossing things in it before dehydrating them. It's just a great super-secret ingredient to save. Feta-wise, I always prefer the creamy Corsican variety. But the stuff sitting in water at the deli is also fine.

Orange-Cumin Vinaigrette

¼ cup extra-virgin olive oil
1 small shallot, finely minced
1 tablespoon freshly squeezed
    orange juice
1 tablespoon sherry vinegar
½ teaspoon ground cumin
½ teaspoon kosher salt
¼ teaspoon crushed red chile flakes
1 tablespoon olive brine

Roasted and marinated root
    vegetables (see page 84)
2 navel oranges, peeled and cut into
    approximately ¾-inch chunks
½ cup pitted black olives*
2 small heads of Belgian endive or
    coralline chicory, trimmed and
    separated into leaves
½ small red onion, sliced as thinly as
    you can
Kosher salt
1 small bunch dill, fronds only
4 ounces crumbled feta cheese

MAKE THE VINAIGRETTE Combine the oil, shallot, orange juice, vinegar, cumin, salt, chile flakes, and olive brine in a small jar with a tight-fitting lid and shake until it all comes together. Set aside until ready to serve or store in the fridge for up to 3 days.

PUT IT TOGETHER AND SERVE In a large bowl, combine the root vegetables, oranges, olives, endive, and onion. Add the vinaigrette and toss well. Taste for seasoning—it might need a bit of salt, but remember that the feta will add some saltiness. Top with the dill and crumbled feta and serve.

*Bonus points for Moroccan oil-cured olives, but Kalamata or Niçoise also work well.

ROASTED AND MARINATED ROOT VEGETABLES WITH PERSIMMONS AND WALNUT-ANCHOVY VINAIGRETTE

MAKES 6 SERVINGS

Here's another nut vinaigrette to add that rich unctuousness to the roots, and anchovies to give a salty, savory component. You wouldn't necessarily taste this and think it's fishy; the anchovy just kind of makes everything else taste better. There are two kinds of persimmons you'll usually see at the market or store—fuyus and hachiyas. You want the fuyus, which can be served crisp, almost like apples. (Hachiyas should feel like liquid in a plastic bag before you eat them, otherwise they're super tannic and basically the worst thing ever—either way, not what you're going for.) Sometimes the skins are tender, and sometimes you want to slice them off. Take a bite and if the skin is just short of shoe leather, cut it off.

Walnut-Anchovy Vinaigrette
½ cup walnuts
¼ cup extra-virgin olive oil
4 anchovies
1 clove garlic, peeled
2 tablespoons white wine vinegar
Zest and juice of 1 lemon
Kosher salt

Roasted and marinated root
   vegetables (see page 84)
2 fuyu (not hachiya) persimmons,
   cut into ¼-inch wedges*
1 small head frisée or escarole,
   cleaned and separated into leaves
½ small red onion, sliced as thinly as
   you can
2 ounces Parmigiano or other hard
   cheese, such as Pecorino or
   aged Gouda

MAKE THE VINAIGRETTE In a food processor, combine the walnuts, oil, anchovies, and garlic and process until smooth. Add the vinegar and lemon juice and zest and pulse two times. Taste for seasoning—if your anchovies are very salty, you won't need any additional salt. Otherwise, add a pinch or so, to your liking. Set aside until ready to use or store in the fridge for up to 5 days.

PUT IT TOGETHER AND SERVE Scatter the root vegetables, persimmons, frisée, and onion on a platter. Spoon the vinaigrette over the mixture. Using a vegetable peeler, shave the cheese over the platter, and serve.

*Pears or figs would work here, too, if you can't find fuyu persimmons.

ROASTED AND MARINATED ROOT VEGETABLES WITH STRAWBERRIES, RICOTTA, AND PISTACHIOS

MAKES 6 SERVINGS

People usually think of roasted root vegetables in winter, but this is a great way to use what's coming up in the spring. Small turnips—aka Tokyo turnips—start popping up right around the time you get strawberries. The tender, sweet golf ball–size beets are at the market, too; and you can pretty much always find great Garnet yams.

Simple Red Wine–Honey Vinaigrette
¼ cup extra-virgin olive oil
1 small shallot, finely minced
2 tablespoons red wine vinegar
½ teaspoon honey
½ teaspoon kosher salt

1 cup fresh whole-milk ricotta cheese
½ teaspoon kosher salt
6 cranks black pepper
Roasted and marinated root vegetables (see page 84)
1 cup quartered strawberries
2 cups arugula
¼ cup pistachios, coarsely chopped

MAKE THE VINAIGRETTE Combine the oil, shallot, vinegar, honey, and salt in a small jar with a tight-fitting lid and shake until it all comes together. Set aside until ready to serve or store in the fridge for up to 3 days.

PUT IT TOGETHER AND SERVE In a small bowl, mix together the ricotta, salt, and pepper. Stir until smooth and creamy. Schmear the ricotta over a platter. Scatter the root vegetables, strawberries, and arugula over the top. Drizzle with the vinaigrette, scatter the pistachios over the top, and serve.

97

5

Panzanella—or bread salad—got its start when people in Tuscany were tossing their day-old bread with tomatoes because they wanted to be able to eat it instead of throwing it out. That evolved into a dish of slightly stale bread that was toasted, tossed with some vinaigrette, and, classically, tomato, cucumber, and oregano.

The first time I was just stunned by how good panzanella could be was when I spent an afternoon in Philly prepping for chef Marc Vetri's Alex's Lemon Stand Charity event alongside chef Chris Bianco. Chris, who is like the king of pure, super-simple food, was making panzanella for a thousand people, and he told me what's key to a great version of the dish: really hard-toasting the bread and soaking it for a long time in a good red wine vinaigrette. You can't argue with that, but I have since added my own ideas; especially after we opened our bakery, Publican Quality Bread, and we had more delicious crusty bread around than we knew what to do with. Because everything's better with toasty, buttery, garlicky bread bits. There's not a whole lot else to say about these recipes except that they're ridiculously simple to make and they put to use flavor combinations that are all great seasonal marriages. Everything just makes sense, time and flavor-wise. Trust me, just make 'em.

TOSS TOGETHER SOME OLD BREAD

To Drink

Serve something juicy and easy-drinking with lower alcohol and preferably with a chill—a Sangiovese from Chianti, a natural Tempranillo from Rioja (but not exclusively). There's also the entire gamut of white, especially Mediterranean island whites that have high salinity, minerality, and acidity (such as Greek Assyrtiko, or Corsican or Sardinian Vermentino). And rosé.

TORN AND TOASTED BREAD WITH PANZANELLA VINAIGRETTE

We figured out pretty quickly that one of the best ways to use our slightly stale bread was to tear it up (instead of cutting it into cubes) so you get these little craggy bits that sop up the dressing; toast it in plenty of olive oil, butter, and salt; douse it with more olive oil or vinaigrette; and toss it with a few simple ingredients to make salads that go with pretty much everything else in this book.

MAKES 4 CUPS TOASTED BREAD AND ½ CUP VINAIGRETTE

1 loaf day-old good bread
2 tablespoons unsalted butter, melted
2 tablespoons extra-virgin olive oil
1 teaspoon minced garlic
1 teaspoon herbes de Provence
    or thyme leaves
1 teaspoon kosher salt

Red Wine Vinaigrette

2 tablespoons red wine vinegar
¼ cup extra-virgin olive oil
1 teaspoon minced garlic
½ teaspoon honey
½ teaspoon kosher salt

or

Apple Cider Vinaigrette

2 tablespoons apple cider vinegar
¼ cup extra-virgin olive oil
2 teaspoons finely minced shallot
1 teaspoon Dijon mustard
1 teaspoon fresh thyme leaves
½ teaspoon honey
½ teaspoon kosher salt

Choose Your Bread

(1) Sourdough's the way to go, or ciabatta, which is a bit lighter and full of air and also a great sponge. That's not to say that a great whole-grain bread wouldn't be delicious, but those are my first choices. And your loaf of white bread is out. Sorry. Basically, the better the bread, the better the panzanella—obvious stuff. And it's not the end of the world if you buy a loaf of bread for this recipe instead of using up whatever's left over. Just slice it up thick and leave it out on a baking sheet overnight to dry out or gently toast it.

Tear

(2) Tear off the crust and set it aside. Tear the inside (the crumb) into approximately 1-inch pieces. They should be rough and shaggy—ready to be doused in lots of olive oil and butter. Then tear up the crust into roughly 1-inch pieces. Repeat until you have 4 packed cups of bread. You could also just get in there and tear up the loaf with your hands instead of slicing it first, but it ends up being more work that way since you have to go back in and break it down into smaller pieces.

Toast

Preheat the oven to 350°F. (3) In a small saucepan, combine the bread, butter, oil, garlic, herbes de Provence or thyme, and salt. Place over medium-low heat until the butter has melted, stirring to mix well. (4) Spoon the butter-oil mixture over the torn bread. (5) Squeeze the bread as you toss it with the oil and butter so that it soaks it all up. Spread the mixture over a rimmed baking sheet in a single layer. Toast for 10 minutes. Give the pan a good shake and continue toasting until GBD (golden-brown-delicious), another 8 to 10 minutes. (6) The bread should be crispy but not dried out and rock hard.

Make a Vinaigrette

If you're going with the red wine vinaigrette, combine the red wine vinegar, oil, garlic, honey, and salt in a small jar with a tight-fitting lid and shake to combine. Set aside until ready to use or store in the fridge for up to 5 days.

If you're in an apple cider vinaigrette mood, combine the apple cider vinegar, oil, shallot, mustard, thyme, honey, and salt in a small jar with a tight-fitting lid and shake to combine. Set aside until ready to use or store in the fridge for up to 5 days.

Put It Together

In a large bowl, toss the bread bits with about half of the vinaigrette and let them sit for a minute or two to soften slightly. Next, dump in your add-ins, taste, and adjust.

Now, on to the add-ins. . . .

TOSS TOGETHER SOME OLD BREAD

PANZANELLA WITH ROASTED LEEKS, PECANS, AND APPLE

Leeks are misunderstood and underrated. A lot of people think of them only as fodder for chicken stock, or they slice them into rings so they just kinda disappear into whatever they're cooked with. But when you cut them lengthwise and roast them in long sheets, they get nice and tender and delicious with really great texture that's perfect for tossing into salads.

Roasted Leeks

2 large leeks, roots and dark green tops trimmed off

2 tablespoons extra-virgin olive oil

2 tablespoons unsalted butter

¼ cup crisp white wine, such as Sauvignon Blanc

1 teaspoon kosher salt

2 cups torn and toasted bread (see page 102)

1 recipe Apple Cider Vinaigrette (page 102)

2 cups torn endive, escarole, or coarsely chopped romaine hearts

1 cup sliced Fuji, Mutsu, Honeycrisp, or other tart green or red apple

½ cup pecans, toasted in a skillet until aromatic

1 teaspoon kosher salt

6 cranks black pepper

4 ounces crumbly blue cheese

MAKE THE ROASTED LEEKS Preheat the oven to 350°F. Slice the leeks in half lengthwise and give them a good rinse—there's often dirt or sand between the leaves. In a large ovenproof sauté pan or small baking pan, add the leeks, cut-side down. They should fit in a single layer without much room around them. Add the oil, butter, wine, and salt to the pan and bake until the leeks are tender and the wine is mostly evaporated, about 15 minutes. Switch the oven to broil. Flip the leeks over and broil until they're golden and charred in spots, 3 to 5 minutes. Let the leeks cool to room temperature, then cut into ½-inch-wide slices. Set aside until ready to serve or store in the fridge for up to 5 days.

SOFTEN THE BREAD In a large bowl, toss the bread bits with about half of the vinaigrette and let them sit for a minute or two to soften slightly.

PUT IT TOGETHER AND SERVE Add the leeks, greens, apple, pecans, salt, and pepper to the bread and give the salad another good toss. Taste and, if desired, add the remaining vinaigrette and toss again or serve the dressing on the side. Finally, add the blue cheese and give it one more quick toss before serving.

105

PANZANELLA WITH HEARTY GREENS, HONEY-ROASTED SQUASH, AND PEAR

MAKES 6 SERVINGS

This is prime-time winter. It features winter squash that's roasted with oil and honey so it gets a little caramelly (it's a bonus that you don't actually have to peel the squash for this recipe), and hearty greens that are a super-strong foil for the sweet squash and pear.

2 cups torn and toasted bread
   (see page 102)
1 recipe Apple Cider Vinaigrette
   (page 102)
1 recipe Honey-Roasted Squash
   (see page 156)
½ cup thinly sliced red onion

1 cup sliced pear (you choose what kind)
2 cups hearty greens, such dandelion
   greens, thinly sliced kale, or
   sturdy spinach*
½ cup shaved Parmigiano cheese**
1 teaspoon kosher salt
6 cranks black pepper

SOFTEN THE BREAD In a large bowl, toss the bread bits with about half of the vinaigrette and let them sit for a minute or two to soften slightly.

PUT IT TOGETHER AND SERVE Add the squash, onion, pear, greens, cheese, salt, and pepper to the bread and give the salad a good but gentle toss, being careful not to break up the squash too much. Taste and, if desired, add the remaining vinaigrette and toss again or serve the dressing on the side.

*Not the baby stuff; it'll wilt too much.
**A vegetable peeler works well here.

PANZANELLA WITH BRUSSELS SPROUTS, GRILLED ONION, AND CRUMBLY CHEESE

MAKES 6 SERVINGS

An old trick I learned when I worked for Rick Bayless at Frontera Grill that I still keep in my pocket is to toss red onions with olive oil, salt, and pepper; char 'em hard without cooking them totally through; and then throw them in a bowl with a splash of balsamic vinegar so they almost pickle. The result is something that's smoky, earthy, rich, and just a little sweet—almost a little meaty. Here I've tossed them into what's basically a version of old-school avec's raw brussels sprouts salad with golden raisins that have been soaked in a little of the vinaigrette, to take off the sweet edge, and a good salty Gouda. But you could also throw the onions on top of steak, with tomatoes in a salad, diced up and tossed with your greens, piled on a hamburger, with the balsamic and the juices spooned over fish. I swear to God, you could add 'em to anything.

Grilled Onion
1 large red onion, peeled
1 tablespoon extra-virgin olive oil
½ teaspoon kosher salt
6 cranks black pepper
2 tablespoons balsamic vinegar

½ cup golden raisins
1 recipe Apple Cider Vinaigrette (page 102)
2 cups torn and toasted bread (see page 102)
2 cups thinly sliced brussels sprouts
1 teaspoon kosher salt
6 cranks black pepper
1 cup thinly sliced or chunked crumbly cheese, such as aged Gouda

109

MAKE THE GRILLED ONION Cut the onion into ¼-inch slices. In a medium bowl, toss the slices with the oil, salt, and pepper.

Preheat a grill to medium heat or heat a large cast-iron pan over medium-high heat. Add the onion slices and cook until deeply charred on one side, about 4 minutes. Remove the onions from the heat.

In a medium bowl, mix the onions with the vinegar. Cover with plastic wrap and let the onion slices sit until they're room temperature, about 15 minutes. Remove the onions from the bowl, discarding any extra liquid, and coarsely chop them. Set aside until ready to serve or store in the fridge for up to 5 days.

SOFTEN THE RAISINS AND BREAD In a large bowl, combine the raisins and about half of the vinaigrette. Let the raisins soften for 15 minutes. Add the bread bits, brussels sprouts, salt, and pepper and give everything a good toss. Let the mixture sit for a minute or two so the bread softens.

PUT IT TOGETHER AND SERVE Add the onions plus the cheese to the bread and give the salad another good toss. Taste and, if desired, add the remaining vinaigrette and toss again or serve the dressing on the side.

TOSS TOGETHER SOME OLD BREAD

PANZANELLA WITH MOZZARELLA, PEACH, AND TOMATO

MAKES 6 SERVINGS

If you're thinking about what's around at the peak of summer, you have peaches and you have tomatoes. They're an unexpected but super-delicious combination, basically because they aren't too dissimilar—they each can be really acidic or sweet.

2 cups torn and toasted bread
   (see page 102)
1 recipe Red Wine Vinaigrette
   (page 102)
8 ounces fresh mozzarella cheese,
   torn into ½- to 1-inch chunks
1 pint cherry tomatoes, sliced in half*

4 large peaches, cut into ½- to
   1-inch pieces
1 teaspoon kosher salt
6 cranks black pepper
2 cups packed arugula
1 cup packed basil

SOFTEN THE BREAD In a large bowl, toss the bread bits with about half of the vinaigrette and let them sit for a minute or two to soften slightly.

PUT IT TOGETHER AND SERVE Add the cheese, cherry tomatoes, peaches, salt, and pepper to the bread and give everything another good toss. Let the mixture sit until the tomatoes give up some of their liquid, another couple of minutes. Add the arugula and basil and give it one more quick toss. Taste and, if desired, add the remaining vinaigrette and toss again or serve the dressing on the side.

*Bonus points for using Sungolds.

NIÇOISE-STYLE PANZANELLA WITH TOMATOES, GREEN BEANS, OLIVES, AND ANCHOVIES

MAKES 6 SERVINGS

I remember making a Niçoise salad for the first time at the first cooking job I ever had, which was at the Metropolis Café in Chicago. I was a young cook, who, having never thought about Nice, France, before, had just learned to make a beautiful Niçoise salad—and it was memorable. It's one of those things that can be so perfect or it can be kind of . . . not. It comes down to using really fresh green beans, or haricots verts, hard-boiled eggs that are cooked properly, roasted (or fresh) tomatoes, and anchovies (which are on my Top-Five Foods list). It's just a great combination, and then anchovies make everything better. You know the deal.

2 large tomatoes, sliced into thick wedges

2 tablespoons extra-virgin olive oil

2 teaspoons balsamic vinegar

2 tablespoons plus 1½ teaspoons kosher salt

½ teaspoon herbes de Provence, or ¼ teaspoon dried thyme

3 eggs

1 cup green beans*

2 cups torn and toasted bread (see page 102)

1 Recipe Red Wine Vinaigrette (page 102)

½ cup pitted black olives, such as Niçoise or Kalamata

6 oil-packed anchovy fillets, torn in half

6 cranks black pepper

2 cups arugula

ROAST THE TOMATOES Preheat the oven to 350°F. On a rimmed baking sheet, toss the tomatoes with the oil, vinegar, ½ teaspoon of the salt, and the herbes de Provence or thyme. Roast for 25 to 30 minutes, until tender and starting to caramelize. Set aside until ready to serve or store them in the fridge for 3 or 4 days. Or, skip this step and use the tomatoes fresh.

HARD-BOIL THE EGGS Fill a bowl with ice water and set aside. Bring a saucepan of water to a boil. Add the eggs, decrease the heat to a simmer, and cook for 10 minutes. Remove the eggs from the water and use a spoon to crack their shells before dropping them into the ice water, which will help the cool water to get between the egg and shell—perfect for easy peeling. When the eggs are just cool enough to handle, peel and set aside until ready to use or store in the fridge for up to 3 days.

continued

*Bonus points for using the skinny ones, which are called haricots verts.

NIÇOISE-STYLE PANZANELLA WITH TOMATOES, GREEN BEANS, OLIVES, AND ANCHOVIES

continued

BLANCH THE GREEN BEANS Fill a large bowl with ice water and set aside. Refill the saucepan with water and bring to a rapid boil. Add 2 tablespoons of the remaining salt and toss in the green beans. Cook until just barely tender, about 30 seconds. Using tongs, transfer the green beans to the ice water. When completely cooled, slice the green beans into pieces and set aside until ready to use or store in the fridge for up to 6 hours, ideally. (You could keep them in the fridge for a couple of days, but they start to lose some of their vibrancy.)

SOFTEN THE BREAD In a large bowl, toss the bread bits with about half of the vinaigrette and let them sit for a minute or two to soften slightly.

PUT IT TOGETHER AND SERVE Add the green beans, roasted tomatoes, olives, anchovies, remaining 1 teaspoon salt, and the pepper to the bread and give the salad another good toss. Let the mixture sit for a minute or two, until the tomatoes start to release some of their juices. Toss in the arugula and taste. If desired, add the remaining vinaigrette and toss again or serve the dressing on the side. Slice the eggs into halves or quarters, set on top of the salad, and serve.

6

I'm a big fan of serving two smaller dishes with one large dish when people come over, and this is a great supporting role-type of deal. Grains are a staple, and they're straightforward—you get what you get. There's a ton of varieties that are essentially interchangeable: farro, quinoa, freekeh, basmati, brown rice. You can make a bunch and keep 'em in the fridge for a few days and toss 'em with a few great ingredients at the last minute. And they're good for ya. So why make grains? Why not make grains!

In traditional tabboulehs, or grain salads, the grains aren't necessarily the star of the dish. There's almost more parsley and vegetables than there is grain. The same goes for these dishes—the vegetables are really what it's all about. So these recipes are driven by what's in your grocery store or market at a given point in time, at the same time.

I could give you a recipe for cooking grains, but honestly, nine times out of ten, we're not going to do better than the directions on the bag. The bag is right. Trust the experts. The one thing I will recommend is that you make the grains ahead of time and let them cool to room temperature before using them in the salads. Any grain you choose can be stored in the fridge for up to 2 days.

MAKE SOME GRAINS

To Drink

Rosé. Or maybe beer—a lager, saison, or farmhouse ale. Or round full-bodied whites, like Chenin Blanc (especially Savennières).

GRAINS WITH BLOOD ORANGES, WALNUTS, AND CHICORIES

MAKES 6 SERVINGS

Cook the grains up to two days ahead and store them in the fridge until you're ready to make this recipe. You could also sear or grill the chicories for extra smoke factor (see "Charring Greens," page 79). Or add other winter citrus. Yum.

2 cups cooked grains of choice (follow the directions on the package!), at room temp

2 blood oranges (navel works, too), peeled and cut into rounds of ½-inch chunks

1 cup chicories (escarole, endive, Treviso, or radicchio), large leaves chopped into 1-inch pieces

1 small red onion, sliced as thinly as you can

½ cup walnut pieces, toasted in a skillet until aromatic

½ cup coarsely chopped pitted green olives, such as Castelvetranos or Lucques

½ cup Italian parsley leaves

¼ cup mint leaves, torn

¼ cup extra-virgin olive oil

1 tablespoon sherry vinegar

1 tablespoon freshly squeezed lemon juice

½ teaspoon kosher salt

6 cranks black pepper

PUT IT TOGETHER AND SERVE In a large serving bowl, combine the grains, oranges, chicories, onion, walnuts, olives, parsley, mint, oil, vinegar, lemon juice, salt, and pepper. Toss, toss, toss! Taste to make sure everything is well mixed and then serve. Store leftovers in the fridge for up to 2 days.

GRAINS WITH ROASTED CAULIFLOWER, BLACK OLIVES, AND ORANGES

MAKES 6 SERVINGS

This is pretty much an all-weather dish, but it's particularly great in winter when there's nothing green comin' out of the ground. Cauliflower is something you can always get at the grocery, and the same goes for olives and oranges. Plus the flavors work really nicely together—starchy, salty, and sweet.

Roasted Cauliflower

1 small head cauliflower

1 tablespoon extra-virgin olive oil

½ teaspoon kosher salt

¼ teaspoon crushed red chile flakes

2 cups cooked grains of choice (follow the directions on the package!), at room temp

2 oranges, peeled and cut into ½-inch chunks

1 small red onion, sliced as thinly as you can

1 small Fresno chile, sliced as thinly as you can

½ cup coarsely chopped pitted black olives, such as Kalamata, Niçoise, or oil-cured Moroccan

½ cup Italian parsley leaves

¼ cup mint leaves, torn

½ cup extra-virgin olive oil

2 tablespoons sherry vinegar

2 tablespoons freshly squeezed lemon juice

½ teaspoon kosher salt

6 cranks black pepper

MAKE THE ROASTED CAULIFLOWER Preheat the oven to 450°F. Place the cauliflower in a small baking dish and rub it with the oil, salt, and chile flakes. Roast until the cauliflower is tender when pierced with a fork and is starting to brown, about 45 minutes. Let cool slightly and cut into bite-size pieces.

PUT IT TOGETHER AND SERVE In a large serving bowl, combine the cauliflower, grains, oranges, onion, chile, olives, parsley, mint, oil, vinegar, lemon juice, salt, and pepper. Toss, toss, toss! Taste to make sure everything is well mixed and then serve. Store leftovers in the fridge for up to 2 days.

GRAINS WITH CHARRED SNAP PEAS, APRICOT, AND MINT

Quickly charring the snap peas keeps them fresh, but takes away a bit of the rawness and adds another layer of flavor, while also adding a little smokiness. A super-springy kinda deal.

1 cup snap peas, cleaned

2 cups cooked grains of your choice (follow the directions on the package!), at room temp

4 fresh apricots, pitted and cut into coarse chunks

1 small red onion, sliced as thinly as you can

1 small Fresno chile, thinly sliced

½ cup Italian parsley leaves

¼ cup mint leaves, torn

¼ cup extra-virgin olive oil

2 tablespoons freshly squeezed lemon juice

½ teaspoon kosher salt

6 cranks black pepper

CHAR THE SNAP PEAS Preheat the broiler to high. Place the snap peas on a baking sheet in a single layer. Put the pan under the broiler, as close as you can get it, and cook for 3 minutes, or until the peas are charred in spots but barely cooked.

PUT IT TOGETHER AND SERVE In a large serving bowl, combine the peas, grains, apricots, onion, chile, parsley, mint, oil, lemon juice, salt, and pepper. Toss, toss, toss! Taste to make sure everything is well mixed and then serve. Store leftovers in the fridge overnight, if desired, but no longer because the fruit and herbs will start to get a little funky.

COOKING FOR GOOD TIMES

GRAINS WITH CHERRIES, CELERY, AND CARAWAY

MAKES 6 SERVINGS

This is an unexpected combination of late-spring flavors that just occurred to me one day when I was cooking at Blackbird. It's a great example of things that happen in nature together making sense on the plate together.

2 cups cooked grains of your choice (follow the directions on the package!), at room temp
1 cup pitted fresh cherries, halved
1 cup thinly sliced celery
1 small red onion, sliced as thinly as you can
½ cup Italian parsley leaves
¼ cup dill leaves, coarsely chopped
¼ cup extra-virgin olive oil

1 tablespoon red wine vinegar
1 tablespoon freshly squeezed lemon juice
½ teaspoon kosher salt
6 cranks black pepper
½ cup crumbled fresh goat cheese or feta cheese
1 tablespoon caraway seeds, lightly toasted in a skillet

PUT IT TOGETHER AND SERVE In a large serving bowl, combine the grains, cherries, celery, onion, parsley, dill, oil, vinegar, lemon juice, salt, and pepper. Toss, toss, toss! Taste to make sure everything is well mixed. Top with the crumbled cheese and caraway seeds and serve. Store leftovers in the fridge overnight if desired, but no longer or the fruit and herbs will start to get a little funky.

129

GRAINS WITH ROASTED CORN AND PEACHES

MAKES 6 SERVINGS

Prime-time summer. Corn and peaches together is one of those combinations that occurs and is just superb. It makes me think about big sun, barbecue, and a time when life was simple.

Roasted Corn
4 ears corn, shucked
1 tablespoon extra-virgin olive oil
1 teaspoon kosher salt
½ teaspoon crushed red chile flakes

2 cups cooked grains of choice
   (follow the directions on the
   package!), at room temp
3 peaches, pitted and cut into
   ½-inch chunks

1 small red onion, sliced as thinly
   as you can
1 small Fresno chile, thinly sliced
½ cup Italian parsley leaves
¼ cup mint leaves, torn
¼ cup extra-virgin olive oil
2 tablespoons freshly squeezed
   lemon juice
½ teaspoon kosher salt
6 cranks black pepper

MAKE THE ROASTED CORN Preheat the oven to 450°F. Place the corn in a small baking dish. Rub with the oil and season with the salt and chile flakes. Roast until the corn is tender and is starting to brown, about 10 minutes. Stand one of the ears of corn on end and, using your knife, cut off the kernels. Repeat for the other ears.

PUT IT TOGETHER AND SERVE In a large serving bowl, combine the corn, grains, peaches, onion, chile, parsley, mint, oil, lemon juice, salt, and pepper. Toss, toss, toss! Taste to make sure everything is well mixed and then serve. Store leftovers in the fridge overnight.

130

7

If you were to ask me what I want to do for a party, my answer would usually be: "Raclette." Or, "Wine, Raclette." Raclette wasn't originally going to be a part of this book, but it couldn't not be included—it completely embodies the spirit of communal eating. It's like how everyone likes Ferris Bueller—the sportos, geeks, and motorheads. Everybody likes raclette. What makes it super-duper magical for me is that I first had raclette on that same trip to Switzerland that completely inspired avec. Verena—Mary's friend from Gais— let us borrow her Volkswagen Golf to drive around Europe. She recommended we make a loop driving south from Switzerland through northern Italy to Provence, hit the Côte d'Azur, drive up the Rhône to Lyon, and eat at Alain Chapel's restaurant in Mionnay, which was the first Michelin-starred restaurant I ever ate at in my life. To this day I could tell you every course I had and how delicious it was. On one of the legs of the trip, we were going to meet a couple that owned a winery called Domaine des Plaines, where they made really great Provençal wines. But we took a wrong turn and ended

continued

MELT SOME CHEESE

up zigzagging through all these small towns in the Alps. We had no GPS, I'm a horrible navigator, and we hadn't mastered the roundabouts yet, so we went around each one three times to make sure we didn't make the wrong turn-off—and it was pitch black. We eventually got our bearings and made it to the winery pretty late. The couple—he was Swiss and she was German—happily invited us in to what was essentially a mini-château and served us cloudy wine samples that they pulled right out of the barrels. And then they asked, "Have you ever done raclette?" Probably the most important question anyone's ever asked me. They set up what was basically a hot plate with little drawers underneath for melting cheese—traditionally raclette cheese, hence the name. It was the best drinking/socializing/food experience that you might ever have. Ever since, we've done raclette almost religiously on New Year's Eve with friends, or other times during the winter because it's really a cold-weather kind of thing. For raclette, you basically take thinly sliced meats—sausage, marinated beef, pork tenderloin—or leftover roasted or poached chicken and give them a nice golden sear on the top deck of the thing, along with any kind of veggies (like scallions, cherry tomatoes, or asparagus) that you can char, too. After that, you cut some raclette cheese into wedges and throw them into these small "shovels" under the top deck. The cheese melts and bubbles and sometimes burns a little bit (which is okay). You dump the bubbly cheese over the boiled potatoes and meat with something a little acidic, like cornichon pickles or leeks tossed in a simple cider vinaigrette. You drink a fair bit, rinse, and repeat. You do it until you're so full that you turn the machine down, continue drinking, and then have a Thanksgiving-style cold meat sandwich later in the night.

To Drink

You're looking for high acidity but still with some body, and maybe a little funky—a stinky wine for your stinky cheese. You've got Frappato from Sicily, Piedirosso from Campania, or any natural reds; Sémillon and Savoie for white; or anything orange. You could go with Georgian qvevri-fermented amber wines, too. Pass on any oak.

here's how

THE RACLETTE FORMULA

Raclette's more about the method than it is the actual recipe—the recipe = method + party + massive wine consumption. It's easy to buy a raclette maker (which is exactly like a double-decker electric Teflon griddle) online; I like the Swissmar brand, and it'll cost you somewhere between eighty and a hundred and fifty bucks.

The leeks are a French bistro classic that are great as an appetizer on their own or served with a slab of pork terrine—or raclette! They're a nice way to cut through some of the fat in this spread.

MAKES 6 SERVINGS

The Necessities

2 pounds red, white, fingerling, or gold potatoes (thin-skinned and golf ball–size)
3 tablespoons kosher salt
2 pounds raclette cheese
2 small jars (or 8 ounces from the olive bar) cornichon pickles

Meat to Grill

1 pound flank, hanger, or skirt steak, thinly sliced

or

1 pound pork tenderloin, thinly sliced

or

1 pound leftover roasted chicken (see page 204), cut into bite-size pieces

or

1 pound kielbasa or bratwursts (nothing too spicy), cut into rounds

Tasty Meat Marinade #1

1 cup extra-virgin olive oil
½ cup whole cloves garlic
2 teaspoons red wine vinegar
2 teaspoons herbes de Provence or thyme leaves
1 bay leaf, fresh preferred but dried works
1 teaspoon crushed red chile flakes
1 teaspoon kosher salt
½ teaspoon freshly ground black pepper

Tasty Meat Marinade #2

1 cup cilantro leaves and stems, coarsely chopped
1 cup Italian parsley leaves and stems, coarsely chopped
1 cup extra-virgin olive oil
½ medium red onion, thinly sliced
½ cup whole cloves garlic
1 teaspoon crushed red chile flakes
1 teaspoon freshly ground black pepper

Marinated Tomatoes

2 teaspoons extra-virgin olive oil
1 teaspoon balsamic vinegar
1 teaspoon herbes de Provence
1 teaspoon kosher salt
1 pound cherry tomatoes

or

Marinated Leeks

2 tablespoons kosher salt
2 large leeks, roots and dark green tops trimmed off, halved lengthwise, cut into 3-inch-wide segments, and well rinsed
1 recipe Apple Cider Vinaigrette (page 102)
1 tablespoon yellow mustard seeds

or

Marinated Asparagus

2 teaspoons extra-virgin olive oil
Zest and juice of 1 lemon
1 teaspoon kosher salt
1 pound asparagus

or

Marinated Scallions

2 teaspoons extra-virgin olive oil
1 teaspoon red wine vinegar
1 teaspoon kosher salt
½ teaspoon freshly ground black pepper
1 pound scallions, ends trimmed

or

Marinated Mushrooms

2 teaspoons extra-virgin olive oil
1 teaspoon balsamic vinegar
1 teaspoon minced garlic
1 teaspoon kosher salt
1 pound cremini mushrooms, halved

or

Marinated Bell Peppers

2 teaspoons extra-virgin olive oil
1 teaspoon red wine vinegar
1 teaspoon kosher salt
½ teaspoon freshly ground black pepper
1 pound red bell peppers, cored, seeded, and cut into 1-inch strips

Boil the Potatoes

Place the potatoes in a large pot and cover with water. Add the salt and bring to a simmer over medium-high heat. Cook until the potatoes are easily pierced with a fork, about 15 minutes. Keep an eye on them—you don't want mashed potatoes. When they're just tender, remove the pot from the heat and drain all but ½ inch of the water. Put the lid back on and keep the potatoes covered in a warm spot until ready to serve. You could make these up to 1 hour in advance or the day before, store them in the fridge overnight, and just gently steam the potatoes to reheat.

Prep the Cheese and Cornichons

If you didn't buy your raclette sliced, cut it into ¼-inch-thick slices and stack it on a serving plate.

Drain the brine from the cornichons and transfer to a small bowl.

Pick a Meat and Make a Marinade

If you're cooking steak, make Tasty Meat Marinade #1: Combine the oil and garlic in a small saucepan. Cook over very low heat (as low as your stove will go) until the garlic is tender and starting to turn golden, about 8 minutes. Remove the pot from the heat and let the oil cool completely. Add the cooled oil, the garlic, and the remaining ingredients to a blender and blend until smooth. This marinade can be stored in an airtight container in the fridge for up to 10 days.

If you're cooking pork, make Tasty Meat Marinade #2: Combine the cilantro, parsley, oil, red onion, garlic, chile flakes, and pepper in a blender and let it rip. This marinade can be stored in an airtight container in the fridge for up to 5 days.

Combine the meat in a bowl with the marinade and set aside at room temperature to marinate for 1 hour. If you're using roasted chicken or sausages, do not marinate.

Pick a Veg or Two

MARINATE THE TOMATOES In a shallow baking dish, combine the oil, vinegar, herbs, salt, and tomatoes. Roll the tomatoes around until well coated. Set aside at room temperature to marinate for 1 hour.

BLANCH AND MARINATE THE LEEKS Prepare a large bowl of ice water with lots of ice. Bring a large pot of water to a boil over high heat. Add the salt and leeks and cook until tender and bright green, 3 to 5 minutes. Strain the leeks from the water and plunge them into the ice water to stop the cooking. When cooled, strain again, and squeeze the leeks dry. Toss the leeks with the vinaigrette and mustard seeds. Set aside at room temperature to marinate for 1 hour or in the fridge for up to 24 hours before serving.

MARINATE THE ASPARAGUS In a shallow baking dish, combine the oil, lemon zest and juice, the salt, and asparagus. Scoot the asparagus around until well coated. Set aside at room temperature to marinate for 1 hour.

MARINATE THE SCALLIONS In a shallow baking dish, combine the oil, red wine vinegar, salt, pepper, and scallions. Scoot the scallions around until well coated. Set aside at room temperature to marinate for 1 hour.

MARINATE THE MUSHROOMS In a shallow baking dish, combine the oil, balsamic vinegar, garlic, salt, and mushrooms. Stir the mushrooms around until well coated. Set aside at room temperature to marinate for 1 hour.

MARINATE THE BELL PEPPERS In a shallow baking dish, combine the oil, red wine vinegar, salt, pepper, and bell peppers. Stir the bell peppers around until well coated. Set aside at room temperature to marinate for 1 hour.

PUTTING IT ALL TOGETHER On page 142, I show you how to finish and enjoy raclette.

139

MELT SOME CHEESE

RACLETTE!

After you've planned, gathered, marinated, and prepared for Raclette (see pages 138 to 139), in the middle of a large table, preheat the raclette grill according to the manufacturer's instructions. Surround the grill with platters and bowls of raclette cheese, cornichons, meats to be cooked, marinated vegetables, cured meats, and smoked sausages. Don't forget the pot of potatoes! When the wine has been poured, start cooking. Have everyone pick what they want to eat and add it to the grill. The vegetables will take 3 to 5 minutes to char and warm through, and the meats will take 5 to 7 minutes to cook. While the veggies and meats are going, tuck the raclette cheese in the warming trays. Cook until the cheese is warm and bubbly, about 3 minutes.

Boiled potatoes (see page 138), warm
Serving plate of sliced raclette
 cheese
Bowl of cornichons
Bowl(s) of marinated steak or pork or
 roasted chicken or sausage

Marinated tomatoes, leeks,
 asparagus, scallions, mushrooms,
 or bell peppers

SET UP Preheat the raclette machine(s). Transfer the potatoes to a serving bowl. Set the potatoes, cheese, and cornichons on the table. Drain the marinade from the steak or pork, if using, and transfer the raw meat and/or roasted chicken to serving bowls; place on the table. Drain the marinade from the vegetable(s), transfer to serving bowl(s), and place on the table.

COOK AND MELT Add pieces of raw meat and vegetables to the top deck of the raclette machine. Load the cheese shovels with raclette and return them to the lower deck of the machine. Occasionally turn the meat and vegetables until cooked or warmed through, respectively. Next, everyone takes 2 or 3 potatoes and smashes them on their plates with their forks. When the meat is cooked and the vegetables are hot, place some of each on the potatoes.

EAT AND REPEAT When the cheese is bubbly and browning on top, everybody uses the plastic scrapers that come with the machine to scoop the melted cheese out of their shovels and over the potatoes, meat, and veg on their plates. Eat with the cornichons. Repeat until stupidly full. Drink some more wine and repeat.

I mean, pizza's the greatest thing in the world, so there's that. Plus I'm always looking for the most efficient way to get delicious things into my mouth, and pizza is pretty much the most perfect vehicle in the world. It's super-versatile and can be as simple as great olive oil, great cheese, and some great vegetables that are in season. Pizza can seem pedestrian, but the same amount of effort goes into a pizza as it does making any other dish in terms of balance and eatability. But more than anything, for me, it's about the flop test—or when you can pull a pizza straight from the oven, lift up a slice, and have it not flop over. It's a tall order—and not always perfectly achievable—but it means that there's structural integrity to the crust and that you're not putting too much wet stuff on top. One thing that's different about the crust of the pizzas in this book: You only add the salt, with a bit of sugar, right at the end of mixing the dough. This helps increase the amount of water you can get into the flour, which ultimately boosts the chewy factor and the crisp factor.

The dough recipe here makes enough for six 12-inch pizzas, but each topping recipe makes enough for two pies. That's because if you're having a bunch of people over, don't make six of the same pie. Way too boring. Make a few of the combinations, and if you're up for it, just put out the ingredients and let people take a pop at making their own pizzas. Or enlist three or four pizza buddies to make all the pizzas with you. Cook off one or two pizzas at a time while everyone has some snacks. Slice 'em, pour drinks, put a nice big salad on the table, and you're good.

MAKE SOME PIZZA DOUGH

To Drink

Rustic, young, inexpensive table reds from Italy—Sangiovese, Nero d'Avola, Montepulciano. No oak, please!

here's how

MAKE DOUGH, FORM A CRUST, MAKE SAUCE, TOP, AND BAKE

This recipe will give you enough dough to make six 12-inch pies, but you can easily scale down to two pizzas or up to make as many as you want. You could also just make the whole batch and freeze the leftover dough wrapped in plastic wrap. To make your life easier, you can make the dough up to three days ahead and store it in the fridge. Anything longer than that, though, and you're in flat, deflated pizza territory. If you don't have a pizza stone or peel, no problem. Just use two rimless baking sheets (or two upside-down rimmed baking sheets)—one that will sit on the lowest rack of your oven while it preheats, and one that you'll flour and assemble the pizza on.

A couple of technical notes: Don't substitute another flour for the 00 flour, or use what might be labeled "pizza flour." The 00 kind is a high-gluten flour that gives you a perfectly crispy, chewy crust. We like the Caputo brand, and King Arthur makes a good version. Also, if you have a sourdough starter, use it for a more deeply flavored crust. Just substitute ¼ cup starter for ¼ cup of the water and ¼ cup of the all-purpose flour.

MAKES SIX 12-INCH PIZZAS

Dough

1½ teaspoons (one 1.25-ounce packet) active dry yeast
3½ cups all-purpose flour, plus more for working the dough
2¾ cups 00 flour
¼ cup extra-virgin olive oil
2½ cups water
1 tablespoon plus 1 teaspoon sugar
1 tablespoon kosher salt

Basic Tomato Sauce

1 (14-ounce) can crushed tomatoes (preferably Bianco diNapoli, San Marzano, or Muir Glen)
1 clove garlic, grated
1 teaspoon kosher salt

About 2 cups of toppings of your choice (assorted cheeses, vegetables, or meats)

Make the Dough

(1) In the bowl of a stand mixer fitted with the dough hook attachment (or in a medium mixing bowl using a wooden spoon, if mixing by hand), combine the yeast and flours. With the mixer running on low speed, slowly pour in the oil. Add the water and mix until combined. The dough will be quite wet.

(2) Knead the dough for 5 minutes with the mixer by continuing to let it run, or turn the dough out onto a well-floured surface and knead by hand for 5 minutes. Sprinkle the sugar and salt on top of the dough and continue to knead vigorously for 1 minute, or until the dough comes together.

(3, 4) Divide the dough into six equal pieces and shape each chunk into a ball. (5) Lightly flour a baking sheet. Place the dough balls on the baking sheet. Sprinkle more flour over the top of the dough and cover with plastic wrap. Let the dough sit at room temperature for 1 hour, or until doubled in size. The dough can be used at this point, but it will only improve by spending the night in the refrigerator. You can keep it there for 3 days before it will be deflated and make flat pizza. If you refrigerate the dough, it does not have to come back to room temperature before shaping and cooking it.

Form a Crust

Preheat the oven to 500°F with a pizza stone or rimless baking sheet on the lowest rack possible. You want your oven to preheat for at least 30 minutes so that everything is good and hot. A hot oven is crucial for a crisp crust.

Dust a pizza peel, rimless baking sheet, or the underside of a rimmed baking sheet with all-purpose flour. Place one ball of dough on your work surface. (6) Flatten the center of the dough using your fingertips, moving in a circular pattern from the center of the dough out

toward the edge. Continue using your fingertips to flatten the dough and form a ½-inch lip around the edge. This will become the crust (or the *cornicione*, if you're fancy).

Continue to enlarge the dough, pressing out from the center until it is 6 to 7 inches in diameter. (7) Here's where it gets a little tricky: You're going to pick up the dough. Let the dough rest over the backs of your hands. (8) Working close to the edge of the dough, but preserving the lip you've created, gently—but assuredly—inch your hands away from each other, carefully stretching the dough. Bring them back together and repeat. The dough will naturally rotate around so that it's being evenly stretched. Continue until the dough is 12 to 15 inches in diameter and very thin. Don't sweat it if you end up with more of a football or amoeba than a circle—I never trust a perfect pizza. And if the dough rips, just set it down on your floured surface and pinch together the tear. That's the beauty of working with a super-hydrated dough.

Lay your dough on the peel and give the peel a quick jerk to do a "check shake." The dough should slide easily around on the peel, which is how you know you'll be able to transfer it to the pizza stone or pan without your fully dressed pizza becoming a crumpled mess. If the dough sticks, gently lift one side and throw some flour underneath. Give it another shake to loosen.

Make the Sauce

In a small bowl, combine the tomatoes, garlic, and salt. You can make this ahead and let it sit at room temperature for a day or store in the fridge for up to 1 week or freeze for up to 2 months.

Top and Bake the Pizza

(9) Spread ¼ cup sauce (Pistachio Pesto, page 163, is pictured) with the back of a spoon up to the lip of the dough. Use the sauce sparingly and work quickly so the dough doesn't get soggy. A huge misstep people make is putting too much sauce on the dough. Don't do it. Continue with any other toppings. Less is more! Quickly slide the dough from the peel onto the preheated stone or baking sheet. Bake for 5 to 7 minutes, until the cheese is bubbly and the crust is golden. Remove the pizza from the oven using your peel or a rimless baking sheet and a pair of tongs. Let the pizza cool for a minute before you slice and serve, if you can last that long.

Canned Tomatoes School

Pretty much every serious pizza guy says the same thing when you ask, "What's the sauce for your Margherita?" Raw tomatoes. Maybe they add a handful of basil or some garlic, but it's always raw tomatoes. It's just good, clean, tomato flavor and it's less gloopy than a cooked sauce. I mean why cook them if you don't have to?

The first thing you'll want to do is make sure you're using tomatoes in juice, not in sauce. Then look for good (preferably Italian) tomatoes, since cheaper ones don't have as much "zing" to them. The higher-quality brands are canned a little bit quicker, so the tomatoes are a little fresher and have more acidity and a richer flavor. My first choice is Bianco DiNapoli (owned by my great friend and pizza hero Chris Bianco), followed by San Marzano and Muir Glen.

The easiest tomatoes to work with are the ones that are already crushed so you don't have to do anything to them, but if you can only find whole tomatoes, just give them a couple clicks in the blender. You could also use a food mill, if that excites you. I highly recommend making extra batches of this sauce, as it keeps for a week and freezes well, and you can use it to do things like braise chicken or toss with pasta. And don't skip grating the garlic—it makes a world of difference.

FANCY BOLOGNA, TALEGGIO, AND CHARRED BITTER GREENS PIZZA

MAKES 2 PIZZAS

PICTURED ON PAGE 170 (LOWER RIGHT). This is major Italiano. Mortadella, bitter greens, and Taleggio—how much more Italian can you get? I would be okay with regular bologna, such as a good kosher version. Extra points for olive pimento loaf. And people are always wondering what to do with the bologna that has the nuts in it—here you go.

Charred Bitter Greens
1 tablespoon extra-virgin olive oil
1 pound greens, such as broccoli rabe, dandelion, radicchio, escarole, or kale
¼ teaspoon kosher salt
1 clove garlic, grated or very thinly sliced
1 teaspoon freshly squeezed lemon juice
¼ teaspoon crushed red chile flakes

2 balls pizza dough (see page 150)
2 teaspoons extra-virgin olive oil
4 ounces fancy bologna, such as mortadella or prosciutto, thinly sliced
4 ounces Taleggio cheese, cut into ⅓-inch cubes
½ cup Castelvetrano (my first choice), Kalamata, or Lucques olives, pitted
2 tablespoons grated Parmigiano cheese

MAKE THE CHARRED GREENS Heat the oil in a medium sauté pan over medium-high heat until shimmery and hot. Add the greens and cook without moving the pan or greens for 1 minute, or until they're slightly charred. Sprinkle the greens with the salt, garlic, lemon juice, and chile flakes. Cook for 2 minutes more, or until the greens are wilted but still have some crunch.

STRETCH, TOP, AND BAKE THE PIZZA Preheat the oven to 500°F with a pizza stone or rimless baking sheet on the lowest rack. Let the oven heat for at least 30 minutes before cooking the pizzas.

Dust a pizza peel, rimless baking sheet, or the underside of a rimmed baking sheet with all-purpose flour. Stretch one ball of dough on the floured peel or rimless baking sheet (see page 150). Spread with 1 teaspoon of the oil and top with half of the sliced bologna, Taleggio cheese, greens, and olives. Get your peel level with the baking stone and give the peel a good shove to transfer the pizza to the stone. Bake for 5 to 7 minutes, or until the cheese is bubbly and the crust is browned.

Stretch and top the second pizza while the first is in the oven.

Remove the first pizza from the oven using your peel or a rimless baking sheet and a pair of tongs. Let the pizza sit for a minute, then top with half of the Parmigiano cheese. Repeat with the second pizza.

SERVE AND STORE Slice the pizza and serve. Store leftover cold pizza in an airtight container in the fridge for up to 2 days.

HONEY-ROASTED WINTER SQUASH AND KALE PESTO PIZZA

A Michel Nischan–inspired special: This one has winter squash, thinly sliced, quickly roasted in the oven, and finished with honey and lemon. The squash is sweet and caramelized and awesome, and it adds really nice texture to a pizza. It's also a great back-pocket item for tossing with some greens, grains, or toasted bread.

Roasted Squash

8 ounces winter squash
    (about ½ medium butternut,
    1 delicata, or 1 acorn)
1 tablespoon extra-virgin olive oil
1 tablespoon honey
½ teaspoon kosher salt
½ teaspoon thyme leaves*
¼ teaspoon freshly ground
    black pepper

Kale Pesto

½ cup extra-virgin olive oil
¼ cup walnuts, toasted in a skillet
    until aromatic
¼ cup grated Pecorino or
    Parmigiano cheese
1 tablespoon freshly squeezed
    lemon juice
1 clove garlic, peeled
Pinch of crushed red chile flakes
2 cups coarsely chopped Tuscan kale
    (ribs removed before chopping)
½ teaspoon kosher salt

2 balls pizza dough (see page 150)
1 cup Basic Tomato Sauce (page 150)
¼ cup walnuts
2 tablespoons grated
    Parmigiano cheese
1 cup arugula
¼ red onion, slivered
Juice of 1 wedge lemon
Pinch of salt

MAKE THE ROASTED SQUASH Preheat the oven to 350°F. Cut off the ends of the squash, slice it in half lengthwise, and scoop out the seeds with a spoon. Cut it into ¼-inch slices.

On a rimmed baking sheet, toss the squash with the oil, honey, salt, thyme, if using, and pepper so it's evenly coated. Roast for 8 minutes, or until the squash starts to sizzle. Stir everything around a bit and roast for 5 minutes more, or until the squash is golden brown and tender but not falling apart. Set aside.

MAKE THE KALE PESTO In a blender or food processor, combine the oil, walnuts, cheese, lemon juice, garlic, and chile flakes and blend until smooth. Add the kale and salt and continue blending until smooth. Use now or store in the fridge for up to 1 week.

continued

*Not necessary if you don't have fresh handy.

HONEY-ROASTED WINTER SQUASH AND KALE PESTO PIZZA

continued

STRETCH, TOP, AND BAKE THE PIZZA Preheat the oven to 500°F with a pizza stone or rimless baking sheet on the lowest rack. Let the oven heat for at least 30 minutes before cooking the pizzas.

Dust a pizza peel, rimless baking sheet, or the underside of a rimmed baking sheet with all-purpose flour. Stretch one ball of dough on the floured peel or rimless baking sheet (see page 150). Spread with half of the tomato sauce, and top with half of the squash and 2 tablespoons of the walnuts. Dollop about 2 tablespoons of the pesto around the pizza. Get your peel level with the baking stone and give the peel a good shove to transfer the pizza to the stone. Bake for 5 to 7 minutes, or until the cheese is bubbly and the crust has taken on some nice brown color.

Stretch and top the second pizza while the first pizza is in the oven.

Remove the first pizza from the oven using your peel or a rimless baking sheet and a pair of tongs. Let the pizza sit for a minute, then top with half of the grated cheese. Repeat with the second pizza.

While the second pizza is baking, combine the arugula, onion, lemon juice, and salt in a medium bowl. Toss to mis.

SERVE AND STORE Top each pizza with half of the salad, slice, and serve. Store leftover cold pizza in an airtight container in the fridge for up to 2 days.

SMOKED WHITEFISH, GARLIC CREAM, AND MARINATED KALE PIZZA

MAKES 2 PIZZAS

PICTURED ON PAGE 161. This is like a Midwestern version of East Coast clam pie, but instead of the steamed clams we're using smoked whitefish. There's no tomato or cheese here, just a garlic-infused white sauce that balances things out with some richness, while marinated kale adds a bright brininess.

Garlic Cream
1 cup heavy cream
3 cloves garlic, smashed in their peels
¼ teaspoon kosher salt

2 balls pizza dough (see page 150)
4 ounces smoked fish (whitefish, trout, or hot-smoked salmon)
1 cup Marinated Kale (see page 86)
4 pinches of crushed red chile flakes
2 teaspoons extra-virgin olive oil
½ lemon, halved

MAKE THE GARLIC CREAM In a small pot, combine the cream, garlic, and salt. Cook over low heat for about 20 minutes, or until the mixture is reduced by half. Keep an eye on it so it doesn't bubble over. Strain the mixture into a small bowl and chill in the fridge for 30 minutes.

STRETCH, TOP, AND BAKE THE PIZZA Preheat the oven to 500°F with a pizza stone or rimless baking sheet on the lowest rack. Let the oven heat for at least 30 minutes before cooking the pizzas.

Dust a pizza peel, rimless baking sheet, or the underside of a rimmed baking sheet with all-purpose flour. Stretch one ball of dough on the floured peel or rimless baking sheet (see page 150). Spread with half of the garlic cream (about ¼ cup). Top with half of the smoked fish, half of the marinated kale, and a couple pinches of chile flakes. Drizzle 1 teaspoon of the oil over the crust. Get your peel level with the baking stone and give the peel a good shove to transfer the pizza to the stone. Bake for 5 to 7 minutes, or until the cream sauce is bubbly, the kale is wilted, and the crust has taken on some nice brown color.

Stretch and top the second pizza while the first is in the oven.

Remove the first pizza from the oven using your peel or a rimless baking sheet and a pair of tongs. Let the pizza sit for at least a minute, then squeeze one of the lemon wedges over the top. Repeat with the second pizza.

SERVE AND STORE Slice the pizza and serve. Store leftover cold pizza in an airtight container in the fridge for up to 2 days.

COOKING FOR GOOD TIMES

PISTACHIO PESTO, ITALIAN SAUSAGE, AND FETA PIZZA

The first time I had pistachios on a pizza—and the pizza that really enlightened me—was at chef Suzanne Goin's wedding at Chris Bianco's Pizzeria Bianco in Phoenix. Chris does this pie that's just olive oil, fresh thyme, red onion, pistachios, and Parmesan. I've re-created it in my own kitchen so many times, and even my not-Bianco version is mind-meltingly delicious. For this version, I took the pistachios and swapped them in for the usual pine nuts in a pesto, along with mint and spinach for basil, which gives you a brighter, herbier sauce that we use here instead of a traditional red sauce. It gets topped with Italian sausage (if you could find a lamb merguez, that would be great here, too) and feta. The effect is fresh and springy. But it could just as easily be served in winter—it's not like you can't find good baby spinach at the market year-round. As for buying feta, quality matters. It's not a food snob thing, it's just that some fetas melt better than others. So you're looking for one that's nice and creamy, not that dry, chalky, oversalted stuff. If the only feta you can find at the store is one that's pre-crumbled or floating in water, substitute a good, creamy goat cheese.

Pistachio Pesto

2 tablespoons pistachios, toasted in a skillet until aromatic

½ clove garlic

1½ teaspoons freshly squeezed lemon juice

2 tablespoons grated Pecorino or Parmigiano cheese

Pinch of crushed red chile flakes

¼ cup extra-virgin olive oil

½ cup spinach

½ cup mint with stems, coarsely chopped

¼ teaspoon kosher salt

2 balls pizza dough (see page 150)

4 ounces ground Italian sausage, browned and drained

4 ounces feta cheese, crumbled

¼ red onion, thinly sliced

3 teaspoons extra-virgin olive oil

1 cup arugula

¼ cup basil leaves, torn

½ teaspoon freshly squeezed lemon juice

Pinch of kosher salt

MAKE THE PISTACHIO PESTO In a blender or food processor, combine the pistachios, garlic, lemon juice, grated cheese, chile flakes, and oil and blend until smooth. Add the spinach, mint, and salt and blend again until smooth. Set aside until ready to serve or store in the fridge for up to 1 week.

STRETCH, TOP, AND BAKE THE PIZZA Preheat the oven to 500°F with a pizza stone or rimless baking sheet on the lowest rack. Let the oven heat for at least 30 minutes before cooking the pizzas.

Dust a pizza peel, rimless baking sheet, or the underside of a rimmed baking sheet with all-purpose flour. Stretch one ball of dough on the floured peel or rimless baking sheet (see page 150). Spread with half of the pesto (about ¼ cup) and top with half of the sausage, half of the feta, and half of the

continued

163

MAKE SOME PIZZA DOUGH

onion. Drizzle 1 teaspoon of the oil over the crust. Get your peel level with the baking stone and give the peel a good shove to transfer the pizza to the stone. Bake for 5 to 7 minutes, or until the pesto is bubbly and the crust has taken on some nice brown color.

Stretch and top the second pizza while the first is in the oven.

Remove the first pizza from the oven using your peel or a rimless baking sheet and a pair of tongs. Repeat with the second pizza.

While the second pizza is baking, combine the arugula, basil, the remaining 1 teaspoon oil, lemon juice, and salt in a medium bowl. Toss to mix.

SERVE AND STORE Top each pizza with half of the salad, slice, and serve. Store leftover cold pizza in an airtight container in the fridge for up to 2 days.

SUMMER SQUASH, FRESH MOZZARELLA, AND CHILE OIL PIZZA

MAKES 2 PIZZAS

I've always loved summer squash; something I learned from my brother, who used to hollow them out with a spoon and pour salad dressing right inside. They're really mild and refreshing and go with pretty much anything, especially on a pizza. You can use any type of squash that you find at the store or market—patty pans, zucchini, summer squash, or even a mix would be great. Squash blossoms would be super-duper great, if you can find them. And then there's the chiles that we use to make a simple infused oil. It's basically pick a chile, any chile. So again, go with whatever's in season and available—Fresnos, cherry bombs, jalapeños, Cubanelles, sweet Hungarian wax. This is a real peak-of-summer type of pie.

Garlic Chile Oil

1 tablespoon sliced garlic
2 tablespoons extra-virgin olive oil
¼ teaspoon kosher salt
1 tablespoon thinly sliced spicy chiles
    (cherry peppers or jalapeños)
1 tablespoon torn basil leaves

2 balls pizza dough (see page 150)
1 cup Basic Tomato Sauce (page 150)

1 medium zucchini or other summer
    squash, cut into ⅛-inch slices
4 ounces mozzarella cheese, cut into
    ¼-inch slices
3 teaspoons extra-virgin olive oil
1 cup arugula
¼ cup basil leaves, torn
½ teaspoon freshly squeezed
    lemon juice
Pinch of kosher salt

MAKE THE GARLIC CHILE OIL In a small pot, combine the garlic, oil, and salt. Place over low heat and bring barely to a simmer. Cook until the garlic is tender but not browned, 3 to 5 minutes. Remove the pot from the heat and stir in the chiles. Add the basil and pour the oil into a small bowl. Let it rest at room temperature for about 10 minutes. This can be set aside until ready to use or stored in the fridge for up to 1 week; just return to room temperature for 1 hour before use.

STRETCH, TOP, AND BAKE THE PIZZA Preheat the oven to 500°F with a pizza stone or rimless baking sheet on the lowest rack. Let the oven heat for at least 30 minutes before you cook the pizzas.

Dust a pizza peel, rimless baking sheet, or the underside of a rimmed baking sheet with all-purpose flour. Stretch one ball of dough on the floured peel or rimless baking sheet (see page 150). Spread with half of the tomato sauce and top with half of the squash and cheese. Drizzle 1 teaspoon of the olive oil over the crust. Get your peel level with the baking stone and give the peel a good shove to transfer the pizza to the stone. Bake for 5 to 7 minutes, or until the cheese is bubbly and the crust has taken on some nice brown color.

continued

SUMMER SQUASH, FRESH MOZZARELLA, AND CHILE OIL PIZZA

continued

Stretch and top the second pizza while the first is in the oven.

Remove the first pizza from the oven using your peel or a rimless baking sheet and a pair of tongs. Repeat with the second pizza cooks.

While the second pizza is baking, combine the arugula, basil, the remaining 1 teaspoon olive oil, lemon juice, and salt in a small bowl. Toss to combine.

SERVE AND STORE Top each pizza with half of the salad, slice, and serve. Store leftover cold pizza in an airtight container in the fridge for up to 2 days.

CHARRED EGGPLANT, SMOKED MOZZARELLA, AND HOT HONEY PIZZA

MAKES 2 PIZZAS

PICTURED ON PAGE 170 (UPPER LEFT). Adding honey to eggplant is a classic Southern Italian thing; it helps the eggplant caramelize more deeply while softening its bitterness. For this pizza, we get the eggplant nice and charred under the broiler, then layer it over the tomato sauce with a drizzle of chile-spiced honey that rounds out the flavor with some sweet-spicy goodness. Glob with smoked mozzarella, melt, and top with arugula and basil salad. Done.

Charred Eggplant

8 ounces Japanese eggplant, cut into ¼-inch slices
1½ teaspoons extra-virgin olive oil
¼ teaspoon kosher salt

Hot Honey

¼ cup honey
2 tablespoons thinly sliced jarred pickled peppers, such as cherry bombs or Calabrian chiles, or ¼ teaspoon ground cayenne pepper
1½ teaspoons water

2 balls pizza dough (see page 150)
1 cup Basic Tomato Sauce (page 150)
8 ounces fresh smoked mozzarella cheese, cut into ¼-inch slices
3 teaspoons extra-virgin olive oil
1 cup arugula
¼ cup basil leaves, torn
½ teaspoon freshly squeezed lemon juice
Pinch of kosher salt

MAKE THE CHARRED EGGPLANT Preheat the broiler to high with your rack in the highest position. In a medium bowl, toss the eggplant with the oil and salt until well coated. Arrange the eggplant in a single layer on a rimmed baking sheet. Place the sheet under the broiler and cook until deeply charred on one side, about 5 minutes. Remove from the oven and set aside to cool.

MAKE THE HOT HONEY In a blender, combine the honey, chiles, and water. Blend on high speed until smooth. Set aside.

STRETCH, TOP, AND BAKE THE PIZZA Preheat the oven to 500°F with a pizza stone or rimless baking sheet on the lowest rack. Let the oven heat for at least 30 minutes before cooking the pizzas.

Dust a pizza peel, rimless baking sheet, or the underside of a rimmed baking sheet with all-purpose flour. Stretch one ball of dough on the floured peel or rimless baking sheet (see page 150). Spread with half of the tomato sauce and top with half of the sliced eggplant and mozzarella. Drizzle 1 teaspoon of the oil over the crust. Get your peel level with the baking stone and give the peel a good shove to transfer the pizza to the stone. Bake for 5 to 7 minutes, or until the cheese is bubbly and the crust has taken on some nice brown color.

Stretch and top the second pizza while the first is in the oven.

Remove the first pizza from the oven using your peel or a rimless baking sheet and a pair of tongs. Drizzle with the hot honey. Repeat with the second pizza.

While the second pizza is baking, combine the arugula, basil, the remaining 1 teaspoon oil, lemon juice, and salt in a medium bowl. Toss to mix.

SERVE AND STORE Top each pizza with half of the salad, slice, and serve. Store leftover cold pizza in an airtight container in the fridge for up to 2 days.

MAKE SOME PIZZA DOUGH

9

My personal love affair with fish started was when I was five years old. Paul Argovitch (no idea if that's how you spell it, but pretty sure that's close), who was the repairman for the refrigeration at my dad's smoked-fish shop, had a cottage in south Wisconsin that he invited my whole family to come out to one summer. I was hanging out lakeside at that house, just this blob of a five-year-old, watching Paul's son standing in the shallows. All of a sudden, he lunged into the lake and caught a giant northern pike. Like, literally plunged his arms into the water and threw that fish onshore. Swear to God; true to life. That night we had it for dinner. Pike's a really bony fish, but Paul filleted it up, cut it into strips, breaded it, and fried it. I know most kids aren't out there falling in love with fish, but I sure did.

continued

ROAST A WHOLE FISH

I've also been an avid fisherman for most of my life. It all started with my Uncle Ben, who lived in Fort Lauderdale but drove to Chicago to pick up me and my brother, then drove us all the way back to Florida, where I cast a line for the first time. Uncle Ben's brother, Uncle Joey (who was a doorman who loved to play the dogs), took us fishing for snapper in the Keys—the first time I'd ever gone saltwater fishing. After that, I pretty much went fishing any opportunity I had, and now I go up to my cabin in Wisconsin and fish whenever life allows. Every chance I get, I'm either sitting in an ice shack with a bunch of buddies and some Busch Light, or I'm out on the lake in an old rowboat, trolling for walleye or muskie, learning to tie knots, and basically trying to wrap my brain around the Zen majesty of it all.

But you came here for the fish recipe.

Serving a fish whole—head, tail, and all—is one of those really impressive-looking things that isn't all that difficult and pays off big time in eatability. You get crispier skin because of the slightly longer cooking time than just cooking a fillet; it's more moist because of all that good, fatty meat that's still in there—especially the belly, which is like unctuous fishy bacon—and everyone can just get in there with their forks (or fingers) and a make a big tasty mess of whatever components you've served it with, whether you're slathering it with a Charred Orange Mayo (page 198) and wrapping it up in Chickpea Crepes (page 198), dousing it in Warm Pepper Vinaigrette (page 193), or giving it a little hot tub of Braised Kale Stew (page 190).

We developed this method for preparing whole fish at avec after we gave a lot of thought to how it's usually served. Most notably, we bone out the fish before we cook it. In just about every country in the world, you get a whole fish and the bones are in it and nobody complains—they just get their hands in there and that's that. But Americans are more persnickety. The other option is usually the very anticlimactic method where you're presented with your roasted fish to look at before it's taken back to the kitchen, boned, drowned in olive oil, and brought back essentially cold. Taking out the bones first helps the fish roast faster, for one. But it also makes it easier to eat. A little work now means people aren't pulling bones out of their mouths at the table—and the smaller the bones, the less fun dinner becomes. Plus we slather the fish in butter before it roasts, which makes up for any of the collagen you're not getting from the bones, and we dredge it in flour (equal parts chickpea flour and rice flour, which add a little flavor while crisping up really nicely and makes this gluten-free for anyone who's asking) before giving it a little pan-fry for the extra-crispy factor and then finishing it in the oven.

Is deboning a fish by far the most complicated thing in this book? You bet. But work the steps and you'll get there. And then you just have to turn around and rub the fish in butter, dredge it in flour, toss it in a pan for a few minutes, and pop the whole thing in the oven for ten minutes—no work at all. All your other components will already be made and can be served room temp-ish or warmed up on the back of the stove while the fish is in the oven. Once the fish is out, everything gets piled on top, maybe you toss together a quick salad, and you're done. You could even bone-out the fish the day before you cook it (just don't butter and dredge it yet). Or I guess you could also just bring this book to your fishmonger and show him or her what you're after with the bones. But, come on, you got this.

To Drink

Old-World Whites—French, Spanish, Italian, Portuguese, Greek. Basically anything from anywhere in Europe that's close to water, preferably the Mediterranean. Even better if they are from islands! Unless you do rosé.

here's how

BUY, BUTCHER, DREDGE, AND ROAST A WHOLE FISH

A 1- to 2-pound fish typically serves two or three. If you're feeding six, we recommend making two fish, and so on. The following fish, as well as any in the bass family, are a good bet: branzino, dorado, bream, black bass, snapper, porgy, or pompano.

MAKES 2 SERVINGS

1 (1- to 2-pound) sea bass, gutted and cleaned
1 tablespoon unsalted butter (salted or cultured is okay, too), softened
Zest of ½ lemon
½ teaspoon thyme leaves, or ¼ teaspoon dried thyme
1 teaspoon kosher salt
Freshly ground black pepper
½ cup chickpea flour
½ cup rice flour
1 teaspoon ground fennel seed
¼ cup oil with a high smoke point, such as canola, rice bran, grapeseed, or peanut oil*

Buy

The most important factor is buying from a reputable high-volume shop. When you get fish at the grocery store, I'd say it's generally been out of the water for five days. It gets overnighted, put on ice, and believe it or not, it's still good about a week later—but not exactly super-fresh. So ask your fish guy or gal some questions about when they get their shipments. Here in Chicago, sea bass comes in from Greece on Wednesdays. It all goes to one distributor, and then it gets sold to a major grocery chain in the city. So I go straight to the source on Wednesdays.

Fresh fish should smell sweet and maybe a little fishy, but have no "off" ammonia-like smell. Clear eyes are always a good sign, but cloudy eyes don't necessarily mean the fish is bad news. (It sometimes just means the fish came up from the depths too quickly.) The gills should be bright red, not brown or green, and the belly shouldn't be discolored. That's where the guts are, so it's one of the first bits that will rot.

Ask your fishmonger to pull the guts out for you, if they haven't already. (That part is a bit messy and kinda gross.) If they're able to, also have them remove the gills. If not, this will be one of your first (simple) steps when you get home.

Butcher

You can use this technique for almost any round fish (versus a flat fish, like a flounder) in the 1- to 2-pound range. Have ready a pair of kitchen shears and a thin-bladed sharp knife. A boning knife with a flexible blade or a paring knife is great—it doesn't have to be fancy, it just has to be sharp. Tweezers or small needle-nose pliers are great for pulling out the little bones (wash before using!).

REMOVE THE FINS (1, 2) Use the kitchen shears to snip off all the fins except the tail. These guys are spiny and will just get in the way when you're eating the fish.

REMOVE THE GILLS (3) Lay the fish in front of you on a cutting board and open the gill flaps (toward the head). You'll see some red, sharp-looking gills underneath. They are connected at the top and the bottom. (4, 5) Use the scissors to snip them loose—two snips and then yank out the gills. You might need a little more snipping to get them free. Repeat on both sides of the fish and don't skip this step—leaving the gills on can lend the fish a livery, bloody flavor.

Rinse the cavity under running water to remove any lingering bits and pat dry.

REMOVE THE BACKBONE Return the fish to the cutting board with the head facing either way and the belly cavity toward you. (6) Grab your sharp

*You can find rice bran oil in Asian markets.

continued

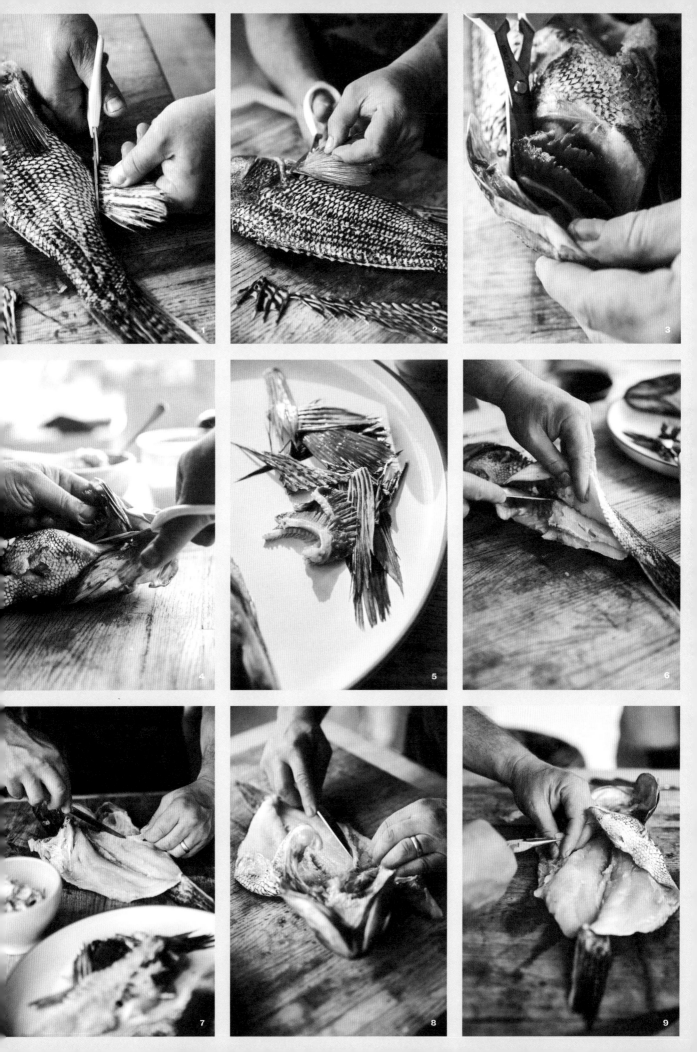

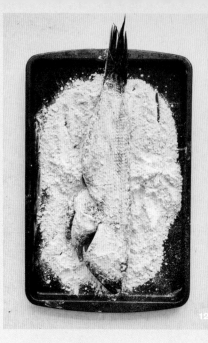

knife. The tail-end of the belly is where you're going to start cutting. Insert the tip of the knife into this spot, keeping the blade parallel to the cutting board. Gently slice into the flesh until you hit the backbone. Continue making small cuts with the knife along the top edge of the backbone, keeping pressure against the backbone until you've gone the length of the fish. You don't need to cut all the way through. (If you do stick your knife through the skin, it's not the end of the world.) Flip the fish over and repeat on the other side until the entire edge of the backbone is exposed. Put down the knife and grab the scissors—use them to cut the bone where it is attached to the tail. Now use your scissors (just the very tip) to snip the bones that run along the belly of the fish. There should be five or six of them along each side.

(7) Drop the scissors and grab the knife! Moving along the backbone again and working front to back, bracing the blade along one side of the spine, make long, smooth strokes to further separate the meat from the bones. Repeat on the other side. The fish should now open completely like a book. Back to the scissors: Cut the bone where it attaches to the head and pull the entire backbone away from the fish. If you cut through the skin, it's no big deal. It just looks a little nicer if you don't. If you want, you could save the bones to use in kale stew (see page 190) or a fish stock; otherwise, trash. Almost there!

REMOVE THE RIBS (8) Insert the tip between the rib bones and the flesh and, keeping your blade parallel to the cutting board, make slices to get to the underside of the ribs. You can do this while also gently tugging at them with your hand to yank them free.

LOOK FOR PIN BONES (9) Run your fingers along the flesh to feel for where the pin bones just barely poke through, and use your tweezers or pliers to gently yank them out. You may need to adjust what angle you're pulling from, but the bones will slide right out. Depending on the fish, there should be 6 or 8, tops. If you can't find them, or if you don't want to, just warn your guests that there will be a few tiny bones. (10) You did it!

Butter

In a small bowl, combine the butter with the lemon zest and thyme. Set aside. Season the inside and outside of the fish with the salt (it's going to seem like less than you think you should use; resist the urge to heavy-hand it) and a couple grinds of black pepper. (11) Lay your fish open like a book and slather one side of the flesh with the butter. (I recommend using the back of large spoon to scoop and schmear so you don't have to dig out any of the butter from the spoon with your finger.) Close up the fish like a butter sandwich.

Dredge

Combine the flours and ground fennel on a baking sheet. (12) Dredge the fish and gently pat it to shake off any excess flour.

Preheat the oven to 500°F.

Fry

Locate an ovenproof pan large enough to hold the fish lying flat. Cast iron is great; stainless steel is great. Nonstick is fine for the timid. Add the oil to your pan over medium-high heat. When a pinch of dredge dropped in the oil starts sputtering right away, the oil's hot enough. (13) Carefully add the fish and gently press the top with a spatula as it fries. (Sometimes the fish will want to open up as it heats.) Make sure the oil's bubbling enthusiastically, but not wildly, and DO NOTHING ELSE. Resist the urge to mess with the fish; the dredge and hot oil will keep it from sticking. As the fish cooks, it will release melted butter into the pan. If the butter starts browning really quickly, just turn down the heat a notch or two. (14) Fry the fish for about 3 minutes on the first side, or until crisp and browned, and then cook the other side. Using oven mitts to protect your hands and arms from the hot oil, tilt the skillet away from you, get your spatula underneath the belly, and carefully lift the fish and flip it away from the oil (toward you). You might also want to ask someone to give you a hand with the pan while you handle the fish.

Roast

(15) Transfer the pan to the oven and roast for 8 to 10 minutes. After 4 minutes, use your spatula to lift the belly flap and confirm that the flesh is turning from translucent to opaque. When the flesh is very close to completely opaque, the fish is done. Even if it's a touch underdone, it'll finish cooking as it cools. And if you overcook it, you'll see white spots of coagulated albumin on the belly, but your fish will still be fine because the meat is really fatty and forgiving.

Serve

All the action with the fish will happen at the last minute, so make sure your other components are ready to go and either at room temperature or warmed through.

A Little Pep Talk

The first ten times I cooked a whole fish as a young cook, I didn't have enough oil in the pan and the pan wasn't hot enough, so the skin ripped off when I tried to flip it. It's something that happens to just about every single one of us, but eventually, we learn that we need to put more oil in the pan and that it needs to be pretty ripping hot. That's a combo that scares a lot of home cooks, and I get that. You have to get past that fear. And in the meantime, you'll have a little salad or stew to throw on top of the fish when you're serving it—so it doesn't have to be too pretty.

WHOLE-ROASTED FISH WITH CREAMY BRAISED BEANS, GREEN SAUCE, AND PICKLED LEMON

MAKES 4 SERVINGS

Shortly after I was named a Best New Chef by *Food & Wine*, the Spanish government invited me—along with other American chefs, including Gabrielle Hamilton, Michael Schlow, Suzanne Goin, and Wylie Dufresne—to basically show off the amazing food the country has to offer. We ate a lot of romesco (which I credit for the dish on page 193), tasted pimentón in a spice shop that carried, like, two hundred varieties, and had some fantastic meals at incredible restaurants. In addition to eating some epic meals and making lifelong friends, we also got to tour the factories where Spain's exported products come from. We saw where they jarred piquillo peppers and white asparagus, and we got to taste all the fish they love to can there—sardines, tuna, clams, mussels. We all fell in love. I remember going to Gabrielle Hamilton's restaurant Prune right after the trip and seeing the menu saturated with those ingredients. I walked away with this dish.

The inspiration comes from *pochas*, a traditional, majorly creamy Spanish bean that we sampled at the factory where they're jarred. (Incidentally, that also became my nickname because, well, I was white, short, and chubby.) To re-create their remarkable texture, we use this cool technique where we first braise the beans, then finish them with aioli, which thickens everything up and makes for the best, creamiest beans—all without having to pay a ton to import anything from Spain. Of course, cooking beans from dry takes longer than opening a can, but there's not much else to this recipe, so it's absolutely worth the extra step.

While this is very much a winter preparation, it's not over-the-top heavy. It gets great brightness from an herbed green sauce (kinda like salsa verde), with parsley, dill, capers, and anchovy. Granted, dill is weird and the last thing you'd find in this non-Italian yet very Italian sauce, but the overall effect is almost like a traditional potato salad with its mayo, dill, and pickles. The pickled lemon, which is like a shortcut version of a preserved lemon, rounds everything out with just a little sweetness, bitterness, and tartness. You can make each of these things ahead (just don't forget to soak the beans the day before you want to cook them), so once you reheat the beans and cook the fish, you've got a meal.

continued

Creamy Braised Beans

2 cups dried runner beans or
    cannellini beans*
1 bay leaf, fresh or dried
2 sprigs thyme
2 cloves garlic, smashed
½ teaspoon kosher salt, plus more
    as needed
2 quarts water
2 tablespoons extra-virgin olive oil

Pickled Lemon

1 lemon, thinly sliced and seeds
    removed
½ small jalapeño chile, seeded and
    finely minced
1 clove garlic, minced
1 tablespoon freshly squeezed
    lemon juice
1 tablespoon sugar
½ teaspoon kosher salt
1 tablespoon chopped dill leaves

Green Sauce

1 cup Italian parsley leaves
½ cup dill leaves and stems
2 tablespoons capers, quickly rinsed
2 anchovy fillets
Zest and juice of 1 lemon
2 cloves garlic, peeled
¼ teaspoon kosher salt
½ cup extra-virgin olive oil

2 whole-roasted fish (see page 178)
1 tablespoon water (optional)
1 tablespoon extra-virgin olive oil
    (optional)
¼ cup good-quality mayonnaise**
½ lemon
½ bunch Italian parsley, roughly
    chopped
¼ bunch dill, roughly chopped

*The fresher the dried beans, the less soaking time they need. If you get dried beans from this year's harvest, then 3 or 4 hours of soaking is enough. Otherwise, overnight is the way to go. I like to buy from Rancho Gordo.
**I like Hellmann's and Duke's.

MAKE THE CREAMY BRAISED BEANS Soak the beans in water in a covered pot for at least 4 hours and up to overnight. Drain and rinse the beans.

In a large pot, combine the drained beans, bay leaf, thyme, garlic, and salt. Add the 2 quarts water and bring to a boil over high heat, then decrease the heat to low and simmer until the beans are tender but still a bit chalky inside, 30 minutes to 1 hour. Before the beans cool, transfer half of the beans and half of the cooking liquid to a blender and blend until completely smooth. Return the puree to the pot and stir to combine. Add the oil and a bit more salt if you think the beans need it.

Continue cooking until the beans are tender but not falling apart, another 30 minutes to 1 hour. Taste to check the seasoning and adjust accordingly. If not serving right away, let the beans cool completely, then store them in the fridge for up to 5 days.

MAKE THE PICKLED LEMON Combine the lemon, jalapeño, garlic, lemon juice, sugar, salt, and dill in a medium bowl and use your hands to mash them together. Put the bowl in the fridge, covered, to chill for at least 30 minutes or up to 5 days.

MAKE THE GREEN SAUCE Combine the parsley, dill, capers, anchovy, lemon zest and juice, the garlic, and salt in a food processor or blender and pulse or blend on low speed for 30 seconds, or until well chopped. Stream in the oil and continue to pulse until combined. Use now or store in the fridge for up to 5 days (it will lose some of its bright green color but will still taste great). Bring to room temperature before serving.

PUT IT TOGETHER AND SERVE While the fish is roasting, reheat the beans in a medium pot over medium-low heat until warm and bubbly. Add the water and oil if the beans look a bit dry. When the beans are good and warm, right before you serve the fish, stir in the mayo with a squeeze of lemon juice.

In a medium bowl, toss together the pickled lemon, parsley, dill, and 1 teaspoon oil.

Spoon the beans onto a serving platter. Carefully transfer the fish to the platter, resting it on top of the beans. Slather the outside of the fish with green sauce, top with the pickled lemon, and serve.

WHOLE-ROASTED FISH WITH SQUID STEW, ROASTED TOMATOES, AND FENNEL

When I opened Blackbird, I pretty much always had this stew on the menu. I wasn't following any particular recipe at the time, but at one point I was looking through one of my favorite regional French cuisine cookbooks (Anne Willan's *French Regional Cooking*—buy a copy if you haven't yet) and realized it was pretty much identical to a classic Provençal fish stew, which is essentially a tomato-based stew that's perfumed with saffron, fennel, garlic, and, of course, seafood. We'd made, like, twenty gallons of it a week year-round, and then stored it in the walk-in and cooked the seafood fresh each day.

What's so great about this stew—aside from being supremely delicious—is that normally a recipe calls for you to make a fish stock first in order to get that base of deep, ocean-y flavor. In this case, the squid does all that work for you. Because it's simmering for about an hour, the squid gets nice and tender while also giving back some of its briny fishiness. You could even throw in more seafood, such as shrimp or a handful of mussels, to poach at the end if you wanted to. And you can use fresh or frozen squid; just not the frozen breaded calamari ringers. I'm partial to Monterey Bay squid, which have thinner bodies and are more delicate and tender than what you get from some of the other guys.

You can store the stew in the fridge for up to 5 days, and it also freezes really well. This definitely shouldn't be the dish you're racing to get on in the morning. Make it ahead, reheat it low and slow while you prep the fish, and take a load off. Then serve with blistered cherry tomatoes you roast alongside the fish and spoon the stew over the top. Done.

187

Squid Stew

½ cup extra-virgin olive oil
1 Spanish onion, thinly sliced
1 fennel bulb, thinly sliced
1 leek, trimmed and thinly sliced
2 shallots, thinly sliced
2 cloves garlic, thinly sliced
2 teaspoons kosher salt, plus
　　more as needed
Zest and juice of 1 orange
Modest pinch of saffron
Pinch of crushed red chile flakes
1 cup dry white wine*
1 (28-ounce) can crushed
　　San Marzano tomatoes
1 pound calamari, fresh or frozen,
　　sliced into ¼-inch rings

1 bay leaf, fresh or dried
2 teaspoons thyme leaves

2 whole-roasted fish (see page 178),
　　prepared through pan-frying but
　　unroasted
1 pound cherry tomatoes**
2 cups arugula
6 large basil leaves, torn
1 teaspoon freshly squeezed
　　lemon juice
2 teaspoons extra-virgin olive oil
¼ teaspoon kosher salt

continued

---

*Choose wine that's good enough to drink, cheap enough to pour in a pot, and has a little acidity, such as a simple Sauvignon Blanc.
**Bonus points if you can find them on the vine.

WHOLE-ROASTED FISH WITH SQUID STEW, ROASTED TOMATOES, AND FENNEL

continued

MAKE THE STEW Heat the oil in a large pot over medium heat. Add the onion, fennel, leek, shallots, garlic, and salt and stir to combine. Cook until the onion is tender but not caramelized, about 10 minutes. If the mixture starts to brown or burn, decrease the heat. Stir in the orange zest and juice, the saffron, chile flakes, and wine. Bring the mixture to a boil and cook until the wine reduces by half, about 5 minutes.

Add the crushed tomatoes, calamari, bay leaf, and thyme. Decrease the heat to low so the stew is at a light simmer. Cook until the calamari is tender, about 1 hour. Taste for seasoning and add a bit more salt if desired.

If you're preparing this in advance, let the stew cool completely before storing it in the fridge (right in the pot is fine!) for up to 5 days, or in the freezer for up to 1 month. Reheat on low.

FINISH THE FISH If you're making this the day you're going to serve it, start preparing the whole-roasted fish while the stew simmers. When the fish is ready to go in the oven, lay the cluster of cherry tomatoes on top of the fish (if they're still on the vine) or scatter them over the fish. Try to avoid putting them directly in the hot oil because they'll splatter. Roast for 8 to 10 minutes. After 4 minutes, use your spatula to lift the belly flap and confirm that the flesh is turning from translucent to opaque. When the flesh is very close to completely opaque, the fish is done. Even if it's a touch underdone, it'll finish cooking as it cools. And if you overcook it, you'll see white spots of coagulated albumin collect on the belly, but your fish will still be fine because the meat is really fatty and forgiving.

PUT IT TOGETHER AND SERVE In a medium bowl, combine the arugula, basil, lemon juice, oil, and salt. Toss to mix.

Pour the stew onto a large serving platter with high sides. Carefully transfer the fish to the platter, allowing any excess oil to drain back into the pan. Add the roasted tomatoes, top with the salad, and serve.

WHOLE-ROASTED FISH WITH BRAISED KALE STEW WITH POTATOES AND SAUSAGE

This is another one of those great winter-type dishes that's super-hearty with the cold-weather trifecta: potatoes, sausage, and braised kale. And yet it's not heavy, and the flavors aren't muddled. You have a ton of aromatics, like fennel, shallots, and leeks, then at the end you puree parsley and cilantro with some of the stew's liquid to make this intensely bright, fresh sauce that finishes off the dish. This is also another instance when I cut corners with the fish stock. Instead, I toss in a couple of anchovies to amp up the fish flavor. They completely melt into the stew, and you'd never guess they were in there, but they have this really nice salty, savory thing going on. That said, if you have a freezer full of fish stock that you want to use, by all means use it in place of water. And if you want to go full-on Portuguese here, finish things off with a handful of clams.

½ cup extra-virgin olive oil
1 Spanish onion, thinly sliced
1 fennel bulb, thinly sliced
2 shallots, thinly sliced
1 leek, trimmed and thinly sliced
4 cloves garlic, thinly sliced
1 small jalapeño chile, thinly sliced
1 tablespoon coriander seeds, crushed
6 anchovies
1 teaspoon kosher salt, plus more as needed
½ cup dry white wine*
1 quart water or fish stock
2 pounds fingerling or small Yukon gold potatoes, cut into bite-size chunks

1 bunch kale or chard, cleaned, ribs removed, and sliced into 1-inch ribbons to make 2 cups
12 littleneck clams (optional)**
8 ounces cured Spanish chorizo, cooked Linguiça sausage, or cooked spicy Italian sausage, cut into ½-inch-thick slices
1 cup Italian parsley leaves
1 cup cilantro leaves
2 whole-roasted fish (see page 178), warm

*For the wine, use something good enough to drink, cheap enough to pour in a pot, and with a little acidity, such as a simple Sauvignon Blanc.
**If you're feeling like an overachiever.

MAKE THE STEW Heat the oil in a large pot over medium heat. Add the onion, fennel, shallots, leek, garlic, jalapeño, coriander seeds, anchovies, and salt. Cook, stirring occasionally, until the onion and shallots are soft but not yet starting to brown, about 10 minutes.

Pour in the wine and reduce by half, about 3 minutes. Add the water or fish stock and bring to a simmer. Decrease the heat to low and continue cooking for 15 minutes. Add the potatoes and cook for 10 minutes. Add the kale and continue cooking until the potatoes are soft, about 10 minutes more. Taste for seasoning, adding a bit of salt if desired. If you're including the clams, toss them in at this point and cook until they're just beginning to open, about 5 minutes. Discard any that haven't opened. Remove the pot from the heat and stir in the sausage.

PUT IT TOGETHER AND SERVE In a blender, combine the parsley, cilantro, and ½ cup of the broth from the pot and blend on high speed until the herbs are pureed, 30 seconds to 1 minute. Add the mixture back to the pot.

Carefully transfer the fish to a serving platter with high sides. Ladle the stew over the fish and serve.

WHOLE-ROASTED FISH WITH ROMESCO AND WARM PEPPER VINAIGRETTE WITH SHRIMP

MAKES 4 SERVINGS

Romesco is one of those fancy words we professional cooks use to refer to a classic Catalonian sauce that the Spaniards go nuts for in the spring when they're all dunking super-charred leeks into bowls of the stuff. But really, it's just a great high-acid, hefty sauce-puree hybrid that's a bunch of ingredients roasted on a baking sheet and blended into a bread-and-nut-thickened tomato–roasted pepper pesto. I like pairing it with an escabèche (again with the fancy words), which is essentially a warmed vinaigrette that's loaded with piquillo or roasted peppers that you can finish off with shrimp, clams, or mussels. This dish gets me thinking about late summer when peppers are out in force at the market, the light is starting to change in the evenings, and the air gets a little cooler—when you can still have a party outside but everyone needs a jacket or stands around the grill warming their hands by the fire. Doesn't get much better than that.

Romesco

1 cup coarsely chopped canned or fresh tomatoes

½ cup coarsely chopped jarred piquillo peppers or charred red bell peppers (see page 17)

1 shallot, coarsely chopped

2 cloves garlic, peeled

½ teaspoon thyme leaves

½ teaspoon smoked sweet or hot Spanish paprika

2 tablespoons extra-virgin olive oil

1 tablespoon Kosher salt, plus more as needed

6 cranks black pepper

1 slice ciabatta or sourdough bread, torn into pieces*

1 tablespoon Marcona almonds (smoked almonds or raw almonds are fine, too)

1 to 3 teaspoons sherry vinegar

Warm Pepper Vinaigrette with Shrimp

¼ cup extra-virgin olive oil

1 cup sliced Spanish onions

½ teaspoon fennel seeds

½ teaspoon ground coriander

¼ teaspoon coarsely crushed black peppercorns

Kosher salt

½ cup sliced jarred piquillo peppers or roasted red bell peppers (see page 17)

1 tablespoon champagne vinegar

4 ounces shelled and deveined shrimp, cut into ½-inch chunks, or rock shrimp; or 20 clams or mussels

½ cup white wine (optional)

2 whole-roasted fish (see page 178), still warm

continued

*Bonus points for using slightly stale bread.

WHOLE-ROASTED FISH WITH ROMESCO AND WARM PEPPER VINAIGRETTE

continued

MAKE THE ROMESCO Preheat the oven to 450°F. Pile the tomatoes, peppers, shallot, garlic, thyme, paprika, and 1 tablespoon of the oil on a baking sheet. Season with the salt and pepper and give it all a toss to coat. Roast in the oven for 10 to 12 minutes, until the shallot has softened. Add the bread and almonds to the baking sheet and roast for another 4 to 5 minutes, or until the bread is golden and the nuts are toasted. A little char around the edges of the pepper mixture is okay.

Transfer everything to a blender or food processor with the remaining 1 tablespoon oil and 1 teaspoon of the sherry vinegar. Pulse or blend until smooth-ish. Taste and, if you want, add more sherry vinegar. Use now or cool completely, then store in a lidded container in the fridge for up to 3 days. Gently warm or let come to room temperature before serving.

MAKE THE WARM PEPPER VINAIGRETTE Heat 2 tablespoons of the oil in a large sauté pan over medium-high heat. Add the onions and decrease the heat to medium-low. You want them just to sweat, not caramelize. Add the fennel seeds, coriander, and black pepper. Season with a small pinch of salt—you're not going for flavor so much as helping to draw out some of the moisture from the onions. Cook for about 10 minutes, or until the onions are tender but not mushy or slimy. Add the sliced peppers to the pan, plus the champagne vinegar and another 2 tablespoons of the oil. Warm the mixture through and adjust the seasoning with salt if desired.

Fold the shrimp into the mixture and increase the heat to medium. Cook for 3 to 4 minutes, or until the shrimp have gone from gray to slightly opaque and pink. If you're using clams or mussels instead, add the white wine, cover the pot, and cook for 3 to 4 minutes, or until most if not all of the clams or mussels have opened. (Toss any that haven't opened.) Use now or cool completely and store in a lidded container in the fridge for up to 3 days. Gently warm or let it come to room temperature before serving.

PUT IT TOGETHER Carefully transfer the fish to a serving platter. Spoon the sauce and vinaigrette over the fish. Serve warm or at room temperature.

ROMP

ROMP (red onion, mint, parsley) is a salad that started as something we served with cheese at avec, mainly because I really love red onions and had to figure out what to serve with cheese. But it's gone on to be one of those workhorse staples that we use on pretty much everything. You wouldn't sit down and tuck into a bowl of this, but you would roast a whole fish and throw this on top. Braise a pork shoulder; you throw this on top. A grilled steak; this on top. Roasted vegetables, or even just great tomatoes—finish with ROMP. It's got such great brightness and freshness from whole leaves of mint and parsley, thinly sliced red onion, olive oil, lemon juice, and salt. It's always been pretty heavy on parsley, but now we've managed to ramp it up (*romp* it up?) even more. Especially with bigger flavors, parsley acts as a cleanser. It's a super-fresh top note, like adding an herb to a salad but on steroids. To make ROMP, stir together ½ cup parsley leaves, ½ cup mint leaves, ¼ cup very thinly sliced onion, 1 teaspoon extra-virgin olive oil, ½ teaspoon lemon juice, and 2 pinches of salt. Use immediately. Makes about 1½ cups.

WHOLE-ROASTED FISH WITH FRENCHY-STYLE TACOS

PICTURED ON PAGES 196 AND 197. The first time I ever went to Europe, I visited Provence. I had convinced the chef that I was working for to subsidize a trip, so Mary and I flew out to Zurich to see her friend Verena (see page 2), borrowed her car to drive down to Nice in the South of France, and then continued down the Côte d'Azur to a town called Saint-Raphael. I was already obsessed with Provençal cooking thanks to the aforementioned *French Regional Cooking*—a really influential book for me as a young cook. But then I got to go and see the markets exploding with things like eggplant, tomatoes, and zucchini (ingredients we got, like, only three months out of the year in Chicago), lavender everywhere, and herb-marinated olives—all those flavors became seared into my being.

This dish is basically a tribute to two of my favorite things: being in the South of France and my absolute love of grilled fish tacos. You could also throw in a third thing, which is broiling fish with mayonnaise slathered over the top. It's a Mexican technique that I first came across when cooking at Topolobampo with Rick Bayless. The mayonnaise gets caramelized and charred, and is just ridiculously good.

A lot of people turn up their noses at cooking with lavender because they think it'll make a dish taste like potpourri. But here it's balanced with the citrus in the mayo and the brininess of the marinated olives. And it all gets wrapped up in doughy chickpea crepes, but you could substitute a good, crusty bread, like ciabatta (see page 44) if you want to make things easier.

Charred-Orange Mayo

1 orange, halved
½ cup good store-bought
    mayonnaise*
¼ teaspoon kosher salt

Lavender Vinaigrette

1 shallot, chopped
½ teaspoon thyme leaves
1 teaspoon food-grade dried lavender
    or fresh rosemary
½ teaspoon kosher salt, plus
    more as needed
¼ teaspoon freshly ground
    black pepper
¼ cup red wine vinegar
½ teaspoon honey
½ cup extra-virgin olive oil

Chickpea Crepes

1 teaspoon herbes de Provence
½ teaspoon kosher salt
2 teaspoons extra-virgin olive oil
1 cup water
1 cup chickpea flour

2 whole-roasted fish (see page 178),
    still warm
2 cups arugula
Pinch of kosher salt
1 recipe Marinated Olives (page 14)

*I like Hellmann's and Duke's.

MAKE THE CHARRED-ORANGE MAYO Preheat the broiler on high. If you have a broiler in your oven (versus below it), adjust an oven rack so it's in the highest position. Set the orange halves cut-side up on a baking sheet and broil until the orange is deeply charred and just starting to burn, about 4 minutes. When cool enough to handle, squeeze the juice into a medium bowl. Stir in the mayo and salt. Use now or store in the fridge for up to 5 days.

MAKE THE LAVENDER VINAIGRETTE I like to do all my vinaigrettes virtually the same way—I chop together all the hard stuff, like the shallots, garlic, and herbs, along with the salt and pepper so it becomes almost like a paste. In this case it's the shallot, thyme, lavender, salt, and pepper. Combine them on a cutting board and mince. You don't want to chop it so fine that you lose all the texture, but you want to chop it pretty darn fine.

Transfer the paste to a medium bowl and combine it with the vinegar, honey, and about two-thirds of the olive oil. Whisk to combine; it's okay if it's a little broken. I like a nice, sharp vinaigrette, but taste and see if you like the acidity. If you want to mellow it out a little, add a little more olive oil. Wait to mix with the greens until you decide whether it needs a little more salt. Use now or store in the fridge for up to 5 days, and bring to room temperature before serving.

MAKE THE CREPES Combine the herbes de Provence, salt, oil, and water in a blender and blend on low speed. With the blender still running, slowly stream in the flour. Once combined, allow the batter to sit in the blender at room temperature for 30 minutes, which allows for the chickpea flour to fully hydrate, giving you a sturdier crepe.

Place an 8-inch nonstick skillet or crepe pan over medium heat. Add 3 tablespoons of batter to the pan, then lift the pan off the heat to tilt and rotate the pan until the batter forms a thin, even layer. Return to the heat and cook until the top is set, about 2 minutes. Flip the crepe and cook until lightly browned, about 1 minute more. (Fair warning: You almost always end up pitching the first crepe; there's some unknown law of physics that says the first crepe almost never works.)

Transfer the crepe to a piece of parchment or wax paper and continue with the rest of the batter, placing a piece of parchment between each crepe to avoid them sticking together. At this point you could store the stacked crepes in the fridge in a resealable bag for up to 3 days. To reheat, warm them quickly in a pan over low heat (about 30 seconds per side) or the oven (on a baking sheet at 500°F).

PUT IT TOGETHER AND SERVE While the fish is roasting, put the arugula, lavender vinaigrette, and salt in a medium bowl and toss to combine. Set aside.

Again, preheat the broiler. Use one long spatula or two spatulas (so the entire roasted fish is supported) to carefully transfer each fish to a baking sheet. Slather the top of both fish evenly with the mayo and broil for 2 minutes, watching the entire time it caramelizes. It's okay for it to get a little dark brown, but you don't want it to burn. The mayonnaise actually will protect the fish from continuing to cook, so don't worry about overcooking the fish.

Carefully transfer the fish to a serving platter. Top with the arugula salad. Serve with the crepes and marinated olives on the side.

10

I could eat chicken twice a week all year—it's my number-one favorite food in the whole world. To me, any time is chicken time; it's perfect any season, any time of day. There's roast chicken and rosé in the yard in summer, served tepid, not even warm. Or in the winter, piping hot with the drippings spooned over a trencher of sourdough. I mean what's more communal and delicious than chicken? If you ask a group of twenty chefs, I'll bet that most of them will say roasted chicken is their favorite, too. I always think people see chicken on a restaurant menu as a throwaway, but the thing is, if you can nail a great chicken dish, it can be the best thing ever. That said, the ultimate whole-roasted chicken is cooked until it's completely done (not par-roasted), rested, and cut up while it's still hot. And the only way to do that in a restaurant is to have people wait an hour and change to eat it after they've ordered it. So to my mind, it's the ideal home-cooked dish.

For me it's The Chicken, and then everything else. So the recipes in this chapter aren't like the braised pork shoulder or whole-roasted fish sections, where other ingredients get incorporated into the dish itself. These are just my recommendations for what's delicious alongside the bird, especially things that are designed to get thrown into the pan during the last few minutes of roasting and take on all the drippings. But quite honestly, I'd be happy with just the bird and skin. Because as many times as the doctor says don't eat the skin . . . you gotta die happy, you gotta eat the skin.

ROAST A YARD BIRD

To Drink

Pour full-bodied, un-oaked white like Sémillon, Viognier, or Chardonnay; or lighter medium-body reds, like anything from Languedoc (Grenache, Syrah), anything funky from the Rhône Valley, or natty reds from the Loire Valley.

here's how

SEASON, STUFF, TRUSS, ROAST, AND CARVE A CHICKEN . . . THEN MAKE STOCK

This recipe is one that I developed a number of years ago after I read an article about Joël Robuchon cooking the way his grandmother did. She stuffed the bird with aromatics and herbs; slathered the whole thing with butter, olive oil, and salt; and roasted it in a pan with lemon, garlic, butter, and water to make a sort of caramelized, lemony gravy that she'd baste with. I've stayed pretty true to this approach, but got rid of the part where you have to flip the bird every which way every 15 minutes. Instead, I cook it breast-side down in the gravy and flip once about halfway through roasting. It's not only less hands-on, but it also buys you some time for getting the thighs perfectly done because it slows down the cooking of the breast and keeps it super-moist. It's just a really great technique that doesn't take much effort. And because of that, I don't like messing with it.

MAKES 6 SERVINGS

1 (3- to 4-pound) chicken
1 tablespoon kosher salt
1 teaspoon freshly ground black pepper
¼ cup unsalted butter, softened
1 head garlic, halved through the equator
1 small carrot, peeled and coarsely chopped
1 lemon, halved
1 small onion, root end trimmed and halved
2 sprigs thyme
2 sprigs rosemary
2 tablespoons extra-virgin olive oil
¼ cup water

Season

Grab any high-sided roasting pan—ceramic, glass, or metal is fine—that's about 9 x 13 inches. Working in the pan, check to see if there's a bag of chicken parts inside the bird, and remove it if there is. (1) Season the chicken inside and out with the salt and pepper, making sure to get in all of the crevices. (2) Rub the cavity of the bird with 1 tablespoon of the softened butter (or mash it in there with the back of a spoon), and insert half of the garlic head, the carrot, lemon, onion, and 1 sprig each of thyme and rosemary.

Truss

(3) This is the trickiest part of roasting the chicken. Start by cutting a 3-foot-long piece of butcher's twine. Tuck the wing tips under the bird. Then find the middle point of your twine. With the chicken's legs closest to you, place the middle of the string at the neck of the chicken. Working with both hands, bring the twine around the tucked wings and to the crossed legs of the chicken. Loop each end of the twine around a drumstick and tie a knot, firmly pulling on the twine to make a tight package. A simple overhand knot works well, but I recommended the hockey skate tie for keeping things extra secure: Just wrap one end of the string around the loop a second time and cinch it closed.

Roast

Preheat the oven to 375°F. Add the remaining half head of garlic and 1 sprig thyme and rosemary to the pan with the chicken. (4, 5) Rub the chicken all over with the remaining 3 tablespoons butter and the oil. Flip the bird on to its breast. Wash your hands! Then add the water to the pan. Roast the chicken for 30 minutes. (6) Remove the pan from the oven, flip the chicken on its back, and spoon some of the drippings over the top of the bird. Return the pan to the oven and continue roasting for another 30 minutes, spooning the juices over the chicken every 10 minutes. The bird should start to take on some color. The goal here is a succulent bird—not a crispy-skinned one. Continue roasting until the bird is completely cooked and registers 165°F on a meat thermometer inserted where the thigh meets the body (the last place to cook, always). Start checking

the temperature after the bird has cooked for 1 hour. Depending on the size of your bird, it might require some additional cooking time. Remove the pan from the oven and let the chicken rest for 10 minutes, spooning some of the roasting juice over the bird as it sits.

Carve

Transfer the chicken to a cutting board. Toss out the vegetables in the pan, but keep the pan juices. Now you're going to cut up the bird into four large pieces with the bones in. With the bird breast-side up, cut between the breasts just to one side of the backbone to separate the breast from the bone. Get the tip of your knife in there (you'll want a durable chef's knife for this) and work from the front to the back of the bird. Repeat on the other side of the backbone and set aside the bone (save it for stock). Take the two halves of the bird and cut them in half again by slicing the legs off the breast halves. Put the chicken on a serving plate and spoon over the reserved pan juices. Eat.

ROAST A YARD BIRD

Jonathan Waxman's No-Recipe Chicken Stock

Yes, here's another thing with Jonathan Waxman's name on it. This time it's an homage to Jonathan Waxman, the Chicken Master. Everyone says his chicken is the best, and ever since he came up to our cabin and made it for us—on the grill, obviously—I can't really argue with that. What stood out to me most about his chicken-cooking routine was that after we'd finished eating, he took all of our plates and dumped every scrap of meat, skin, and bone, along with the drippings from the roasting pan, into a big pot with water and let it simmer really low overnight to make a rich but totally easy stock that sort of defies what people assume has to be involved with making it. There's no real recipe, just combine the scraps, bones, and drippings in a stockpot; fill with water; bring just to a boil; and simmer on low, covered, for 12 hours. Strain into a clean container, skim the fat off the surface, and store in the fridge for up to 1 week or in the freezer for up to 1 month.

ROASTED CHICKEN WITH ROASTED GRAPES AND VETRI'S FENNEL

MAKES 6 SERVINGS

PICTURED ON PAGES 208 AND 209. I saw Marc Vetri make fennel this way once, and it really stuck with me because it is so simple but turns fennel—which can be a little divisive if you don't like its anise-y flavor—into something really rich and balanced. He took thin wedges of the bulb and quickly roasted them with olive oil and a ton of Parmesan cheese on top—which basically becomes a gratin. It's super-good with the chicken as a slightly sweet, earthy counterpart. Roasted grapes are a typical French accompaniment to poultry—pigeon, quail, etc.—so I like tossing in a few clusters on the stem at the end of roasting. As excited as I get about local varieties when they're in season in the late summer/fall (Jupiters, Concords), and as wacky awesome as something like champagne grapes would be here, I'm pretty much just as happy with good ol' fair-trade red seedless grapes from the grocery store.

3 medium or 2 large bulbs fennel, cut into ¼-inch wedges
½ cup plus 2 tablespoons extra-virgin olive oil
½ cup freshly grated Parmigiano cheese
1 teaspoon kosher salt
½ teaspoon freshly ground black pepper

1 pound red seedless grapes on the stem, divided into small clusters (4 to 7 grapes each)
1 roasted chicken (see page 204), warm
Dill fronds

207

ROAST THE FENNEL Preheat the oven to 375°F. Arrange the fennel in a single layer on a small rimmed baking sheet or in a roasting pan. Add enough of the oil so that it comes about halfway up the side of the fennel (you will need about ½ cup). Cover the fennel evenly with the cheese, ½ teaspoon of the salt, and ¼ teaspoon of the pepper. Roast until the fennel is tender, 15 to 20 minutes.

ROAST THE GRAPES Arrange the grapes in a single layer in a small baking dish. Drizzle with the remaining 2 tablespoons oil, the remaining ½ teaspoon salt, and remaining ¼ teaspoon pepper. Roast until the grapes start to soften and a couple have burst, 8 minutes, maybe a little longer (it'll depend on how big your grapes are). You could also just toss the grapes in the pan with the chicken during the final 8 minutes of cooking.

PUT IT TOGETHER AND SERVE Carve the chicken (see page 205) and arrange on a platter. Tuck the fennel around the chicken and pour its roasting oil over the platter. Top with the grapes and dill.

ROASTED CHICKEN WITH ROASTED MUSHROOM TRENCHERS AND ROSEMARY

MAKES 6 SERVINGS

PICTURED ON PAGE 213. This goes back to the whole idea of bread being the essential vehicle for getting all the delicious juices into your mouth. I personally think a nice, thick piece of sourdough—aka a trencher—that you spoon the roasted chicken drippings onto and crisp up in the oven sounds pretty good as the bed for the roasted chicken, along with a whole bunch of mushrooms that have been sautéed in olive oil and garlic. Yeah, you can get fancy with the mushrooms—and yes, chanterelles are pretty darn tasty—but I'm a cremini fan. I like their chunky texture. They've got great mushroomy flavor, and they're cheap! When I was a kid, the big treat was driving to a place called the Wagon Wheel, where the specialty was deep-fried cremini. And then there was my grandma, who, when she wasn't making pigs in a blanket for the Jewish holidays, would cook some creminis in oil and garlic and wrap them up in Hungry Jack biscuit dough. Both are among the greatest things a human being can eat, and both are proof that creminis are totally underrated. Even though I think a perfectly roasted chicken is pretty hard to improve on, in this case we added a simple pan sauce that uses the caramelized, cooked-down lemon and garlic from the finished chicken along with the garlic and rosemary from the mushrooms, plus a little butter, for good measure.

2 tablespoons extra-virgin olive oil
1 pound mushrooms, such as cremini, oyster, or shiitake, cleaned and cut into slightly larger than bite-size chunks
4 cloves garlic, peeled and crushed
1 large sprig rosemary
½ teaspoon freshly ground black pepper

1 teaspoon kosher salt
1 roasted chicken (see page 204), warm
1 cup chicken stock*
Juice of ½ lemon
2 tablespoons unsalted butter
1 or 2 lengthwise slices of rustic bread, such as ciabatta or sourdough

*Can be store-bought, but homemade stuff is the best. See page 206 if you need convincing on how easy it is to make.

COOK THE MUSHROOMS Heat a large sauté pan (cast iron is great here) over medium-high heat. Add the oil and when it starts to shimmer or barely smoke, add the mushrooms so they sit in a single layer. Toss in the garlic, rosemary, and ¼ teaspoon of the pepper and cook without stirring until the mushrooms are browned on one side and are giving up their liquid, about 5 minutes. Season with ½ teaspoon of the salt and give the pan a good shake. Cook for 1 minute more. Remove the pan from the heat and reserve in a warm spot until the chicken is ready.

MAKE THE PAN SAUCE When the chicken comes out of the oven and is resting, reserve a couple tablespoons of the drippings. Combine the chicken stock with the crushed garlic and rosemary from the mushroom pan, along with any lemon or garlic bits you can scrape out of the chicken pan. Bring the stock to a boil, decrease the heat to a simmer, and cook until reduced by two-thirds, 6 to 8 minutes. Stir in the lemon juice, butter, and the remaining ½ teaspoon salt and ¼ teaspoon pepper. Continue simmering until the butter has melted and the sauce has thickened slightly, another 5 minutes.

PUT IT TOGETHER Carve the chicken (see page 205) while the sauce is reducing. Drizzle the bread with the reserved drippings and toast in the oven until crisp, about 5 minutes. Place the bread on a platter and top with the mushrooms and carved chicken. Pour over the pan sauce and serve.

ROASTED CHICKEN WITH SMASHED AND CRISPED POTATOES AND GREEN SAUCE #1*

MAKES 6 SERVINGS

We did these potatoes in our last cookbook, and they're perfect with chicken, so here they are again. They're known in some parts of the globe as Waxman Potatoes, thanks again to Jonathan Waxman, and they get boiled, smashed, and crisped in a bunch of olive oil. What's to improve on?

Waxman likes serving these guys with salsa verde, a sauce that's bright, briny, and a little funky from the capers and anchovy. Unlike some restaurants where the salsa verde is a smooth green puree, ours is not. Ours is basically a chunky green relish that just gets chopped up on a board or in a food processor.

Green Sauce #1

1 bunch Italian parsley, leaves and some stems
1 tablespoon salt-packed capers, quickly rinsed
2 cloves garlic, peeled
2 anchovy fillets
Zest and juice of 1 lemon
½ cup extra-virgin olive oil
Kosher salt

Smashed and Crisped Potatoes

2 pounds thin-skinned potatoes, such as Yukon gold
2 tablespoons plus 1 teaspoon kosher salt
¼ cup extra-virgin olive oil

1 roasted chicken (see page 204), warm

MAKE THE GREEN SAUCE In a food processor (or with a mortar and pestle), combine the parsley, capers, garlic, anchovies, and lemon zest. Process until the parsley is roughly chopped. Stir in the lemon juice and oil. Taste and add salt if necessary (usually not needed because the capers and anchovies are salty).

MAKE THE SMASHED POTATOES Place the potatoes and 2 tablespoons of the salt in a stockpot. Cover with cold water by 2 inches. Bring to a simmer over medium-high heat and cook until the potatoes are just barely tender when pierced with a fork. This usually takes 10 to 15 minutes, but start checking at 10 minutes. They should feel a bit firm—not quite mashable. Drain off the water and let the potatoes cool. This can be done ahead and the potatoes can be stored in the refrigerator for up to 5 days.

When you are ready to finish the potatoes, use the palm of your hand to smash them gently. You want to expose the flesh but not smash the potatoes to bits.

Heat a large sauté pan over medium-high heat. Add the oil and, working in batches if necessary, add the potatoes in a single layer. Season with the remaining 1 teaspoon salt and cook until the potatoes are golden brown on both sides, about 5 minutes a side.

PUT IT TOGETHER AND SERVE Carve the chicken (see page 205) and transfer to a serving platter. Place the potatoes around the chicken pieces, drizzle with about ½ cup of the green sauce, and serve.

COOKING FOR GOOD TIMES

*Super-delicious alert.

ROASTED CHICKEN WITH PICKLED SUMMER SQUASH AND SALSA MACHA

MAKES 6 SERVINGS

I think every one of our restaurants has stolen this recipe and just called it something else. The inspiration, which is a sweet, hot, chunky, oily, black tar–like salsa made with all kinds of dried chiles and no tomato or tomatillos, actually comes from El Barco, a mariscos restaurant here in Chicago on Ashland Avenue that serves it with chips. Here, the salsa works really nicely with pickled summer squash because it's more like a bread-and-butter-style pickle with that sweet-sour thing happening. The overall effect is a great warm-weather treatment for a whole roast bird.

Salsa Macha

1 cup extra-virgin olive oil
¼ cup almonds
8 cloves garlic, peeled
1 tablespoon sesame seeds
3 dried árbol chiles, seeded and stemmed
2 dried ancho chiles, seeded and stemmed
2 dried guajillo chiles, seeded and stemmed
1 tablespoon white wine vinegar or apple cider vinegar
1 teaspoon sugar
2 teaspoons kosher salt

Pickled Summer Squash

1 pound summer squash (zucchini, yellow squash, or pattypan), cut into ⅛-inch-wide slices
1 small red onion, cut into ⅛-inch-wide slices
2 tablespoons kosher salt
1 cup apple cider vinegar
⅔ cup sugar
2 teaspoons whole yellow mustard seeds
1 teaspoon ground turmeric
1 teaspoon whole black peppercorns

1 roasted chicken (see page 204), warm

MAKE THE SALSA In a small pot, combine the oil, almonds, and garlic. Gently heat over medium-low heat until the oil bubbles and the garlic is toasted and golden brown, about 10 minutes. Decrease the heat to low and add the sesame seeds and chiles. Cook for 5 minutes. Remove from the heat and allow the mixture to cool to room temperature. Transfer the oil to a blender with the white wine vinegar or apple cider vinegar, sugar, and salt and blend until smooth. This will make more than you need for the recipe, but it's delicious on almost anything—eggs, roasted vegetables, hummus—and will keep in the fridge for up to 5 days.

MAKE THE PICKLED SQUASH In a large bowl, combine the squash, onion, salt, and enough ice water to cover the squash. Give everything a gentle toss and let the squash sit for 30 minutes. Drain the ice water and discard the ice. Set aside.

In a small pot, combine the apple cider vinegar, sugar, mustard seeds, turmeric, and peppercorns and bring to a boil over medium-high heat. Remove the pot from the heat and cool to room temperature. Pour the pickling liquid over the squash and let sit for 1 hour at room temperature or in the refrigerator for up to 5 days.

PUT IT TOGETHER AND SERVE Carve the chicken (see page 205) and transfer to a serving platter. Pour the salsa over the top, tuck in the squash on the side, and serve.

ROASTED CHICKEN WITH CELERY ROOT, APPLES, AND LYDIA'S FAMOUS BUTTERMILK DRESSING

MAKES 6 SERVINGS

Great Lake Pizza is one of those places that if you didn't get to go when it was open, you're really bummed out. It was on a little side street in Andersonville and was owned by a couple, Lydia Esparza and Nick Lessins. It maybe sat twelve people and probably had the greatest pizza that I ever tasted. It was open only four days a week, and Nick only made a certain amount of dough every night, so when they were out, they were out. He made all the pizzas himself without any help, and made them with so much love that they took a little bit more time than you'd expect so you'd always have to wait—but it was worth it. They used all organic ingredients from the Midwest, and the crust was the perfect balance of crunchy-meets-chewy. I mean, I took chef Marc Vetri there, and his jaw just dropped. When we worked on pizza for our latest restaurant, Pacific Standard Time, that was the benchmark. Lydia would always do a seasonal salad or two, and when I took Mary once in the fall, Lydia was doing a celery root salad with this really garlicky, I mean almost overly garlicky, buttermilk dressing. This dish is my homage to that, plus you get all the chicken stuff mixing with the creamy stuff and it's just out of this world.

Lydia's Famous Buttermilk Dressing

1 cup buttermilk (good-quality, thick stuff)
½ cup mayonnaise*
1 tablespoon extra-virgin olive oil
2 tablespoons finely chopped Italian parsley
2 tablespoons minced garlic
2 tablespoons freshly squeezed lemon juice
½ teaspoon kosher salt
6 cranks black pepper

1 large celery root, peeled and cut into ⅛-inch-wide slices
2 tart, crisp apples, cut into ⅛-inch-wide slices
1 roasted chicken (see page 204), warm

MAKE THE DRESSING In a small bowl, combine the buttermilk, mayo, oil, parsley, garlic, lemon juice, salt, and pepper and give the mixture a good whisking.

DRESS THE SALAD In a medium bowl, combine the celery root and apples and toss with enough dressing to just coat (not drown) them. Transfer the remaining dressing to a serving bowl.

PUT IT TOGETHER AND SERVE Carve the chicken (see page 205) and transfer to a serving platter. Spoon the salad over the chicken and serve with the rest of the dressing on the side for dipping.

*I like Hellmann's and Duke's.

11

Braised pork shoulder is avec's OG; it's been on the menu since the very beginning. It's a recipe that Koren Grieveson, the original chef at avec, and I developed. It's reminiscent of a great pot roast— super-juicy, super-succulent—but the first inspiration came from Switzerland, where things would be cooking on the fire and served directly out of the pot that they were made in, family-style. We still follow this approach, cooking and serving the shoulder—which for me is the ultimate soulful hunk of meat to braise—in these cast-iron Staub dishes (that we call *bastards* because they are always burning you), but you could obviously do this in a Dutch oven–type pot, or in lieu of that, any pot with a decently tight-fitting lid. The process is pretty straightforward and typical of a braise: You brine the shoulder to help lock in moisture (as fatty as pork shoulder is, it can still get dry when you braise it), rub it down with salt and paprika, and then simmer it with the usual carrots, onions, fennel, bay, and thyme plus sherry vinegar and honey for a little sweetness and sharpness. Next, you can toss in things like couscous or clams or white beans or greens to simmer with the meat and then serve it with a handful of other ingredients that speak to traditional combinations and the seasons but still let the pork be the star of the show. You can also braise the meat ahead of time, a step I highly recommend because when the fat cools, it rises to the top and then you can just pull that cap off and throw it in with your roasting potatoes.

BRAISE A PORK SHOULDER

To Drink

You want a wine with high fruit and juiciness but some earthiness too, like just about any Iberian Peninsula or Italian red, or anything from southern France, especially Bandol and Roussillon.

here's how

BRINED AND BRAISED PORK SHOULDER

This is definitely an "abundanza" dish—and that's the idea. Hearty and satisfying. Just a couple things to note: Ask your butcher for a leaner shoulder since you're braising and not grinding (a really fatty shoulder is perfect for sausage, just FYI), and feel free to braise the meat up to 5 days in advance. Just store it in its liquid (refrigerated) until you're ready to reheat, then you're in business.

MAKES 6 SERVINGS

1 (3- to 4-pound) pork shoulder

Brine

½ cup kosher salt
¼ cup sugar
2 tablespoons black peppercorns
1 teaspoon crushed red chile flakes
2 fresh bay leaves, or 1 dried
8 sprigs thyme
1 small onion, quartered
2 quarts water

1 tablespoon kosher salt
1 tablespoon smoked paprika
1 small onion, thinly sliced
1 carrot, peeled and thinly sliced
1 stalk fennel, thinly sliced*
6 cloves garlic, smashed
1 small bunch thyme
1 bay leaf, fresh or dried
¼ cup tomato paste
1 cup crisp and cheap white wine
2 tablespoons honey
2 tablespoons sherry vinegar
About 1 quart chicken stock (see page 206)
    or water, plus more as needed

Prep the Pork

(1, 2) Trim the excess fat from the pork shoulder. Cut the meat away from the bone. Roll the meat into a bundle and tie with butcher's twine to secure.

*Save the bulb for something else!

Brine the Pork

MAKE THE BRINE In a stockpot, combine the salt, sugar, peppercorns, chile flakes, bay leaves, thyme, and onion with the water and bring to a boil over high heat. Remove the pot from the heat and let the brine cool completely. Transfer the brine to a large bowl.

(3) Submerge the pork shoulder in the brine and let sit in the fridge overnight. If you can't fit a large pot in your fridge, do what chef Perry Hendrix's dad does and clean out a crisper drawer in the fridge and put the brine right in there. True story.

Preheat the oven to 325°F. (4, 5) Remove the pork shoulder from the brine and rub it down with the salt and paprika. (No need to wipe it off first.)

(6) Combine the pork shoulder with the vegetables and herbs in a large Dutch oven, large pot with lid, or deep roasting pan. Pick a cooking vessel that is big enough to hold everything, but not so big you need a gallon of stock to reach three-quarters of the way up the shoulder to keep the pork moist as it cooks.

In a small bowl, whisk together the tomato paste, wine, honey, and vinegar. Pour the mixture over the pork.

Add enough stock to come up to the "shoulders" of the shoulder. Cover the pork tightly with the lid or seal with two pieces of foil.

Cook for 6 hours, or until the pork is very tender but not totally falling apart. Remove the bay leaves and thyme branches.

The pork can be served straight from the oven, or it can be chilled completely, refrigerated for up to 5 days, and then reheated in a 350°F oven for 45 minutes, or until bubbly and warm in the middle. Either way, it's key to let the pork cool in its braising juices because it'll reabsorb them as it cools.

BRINED AND BRAISED PORK SHOULDER WITH WHITE BEANS, CHORIZO, AND CIDER

MAKES 6 SERVINGS

Braised pork shoulder's flavor is pretty rich and straightforward, so I like serving it with ingredients that add a little dimension. The chorizo is about heat, while the cider adds sweetness and acidity. You can use one of any number of bean varieties, like white runner bean, giant Peruvian lima, great Northern, or cannellini. Super-bonus points for using fresh shelling beans. And if using canned is the difference between making this dish or not, use canned.

White Beans

¼ cup extra-virgin olive oil

8 ounces Spanish dry chorizo, cut into ¼-inch-wide slices

1 large Spanish onion, diced

2 tart apples, such as Granny Smith, diced

4 cloves garlic, thinly sliced

1 tablespoon smoked paprika

2 teaspoons kosher salt, plus more as needed

1 cup hard cider*

1 pound dried white beans, soaked overnight and drained, or 2 (15.5-ounce) cans white beans, such as cannellini or butter

1 brined and braised pork shoulder (see page 224), in its braising liquid

1 tart apple, such as Granny Smith, thinly sliced

½ cup Italian parsley leaves

1 teaspoon freshly squeezed lemon juice

2 teaspoons extra-virgin olive oil

¼ teaspoon kosher salt

MAKE THE BEANS Heat the oil in a medium saucepan over medium heat. Add the chorizo, onion, apples, garlic, paprika, and salt. Cook for about 10 minutes, or until the vegetables are soft but not browning.

Increase the heat to medium-high. When the onion starts to color, pour in the cider. Cook until the cider reduces almost entirely, about 2 minutes. Add the soaked beans to the pot with enough water to cover by 1 inch, about 1 quart. Cook over medium heat until the beans are tender, about 45 minutes. If using canned beans, just add the liquid from the can and cook for 15 to 20 minutes, or until the liquid reduces a bit and everything is delicious.

Taste and season with more salt, if necessary—usually an additional 1 teaspoon for the dry beans and less for canned beans if they are already salted.

PUT IT TOGETHER AND SERVE Preheat the oven to 350°F. If reheating the pork shoulder, cook, covered, until bubbly and warm in the middle, about 45 minutes. Add the beans to the pot and continue cooking, uncovered, until the beans and cooking liquid are bubbling and a little reduced, an additional 20 minutes. (If you're not reheating the pork and making this all in one go, just add the beans during the last 20 minutes of braising.)

In a medium bowl, toss together the apple, parsley, lemon juice, oil, and salt. Top the pork and beans with the salad and serve out of the pot.

*Preferably a dry, funky Spanish cider, but a high-acid wine such as Sauvignon Blanc will also work.

BRINED AND BRAISED PORK SHOULDER WITH KIELBASA SAUSAGE AND BRAISED GREENS

MAKES 6 SERVINGS

I fell in love with long-cooked collards in the South. Then I had a line cook teach me how his grandmother made greens, and ever since it's been the only way I've ever made them. It basically just involves a lot of sugar and vinegar and pork. The greens get super-silky, and you can't beat pork on pork.

Greens

2 bunches collard greens or other sturdy braising greens, such as kale or chard
2 tablespoons extra-virgin olive oil
1 Spanish onion, diced
2 teaspoons kosher salt
¼ cup packed dark brown sugar
¼ cup sherry vinegar
1 cup reserved pork cooking liquid (see page 224), chicken stock (see page 206), or water
1 pound kielbasa sausage or other smoked sausage

1 brined and braised pork shoulder (see page 224), in its braising liquid
1 small red onion, thinly sliced
½ cup Italian parsley leaves
1 cup torn and toasted bread crumbs (see page 102)
1 teaspoon freshly squeezed lemon juice
2 teaspoons extra-virgin olive oil
¼ teaspoon kosher salt

MAKE THE GREENS Clean the collard greens by removing the middle rib of each leaf. Tear each leaf into 2- to 3-inch pieces. Fill a large bowl or pot with cold water, add the leaves, and wash them thoroughly—collards are notoriously sandy. Pat dry and set aside.

Heat the oil in a medium pot over medium heat. Add the onion and salt and cook until the onion is tender, about 10 minutes. Add the brown sugar and vinegar and cook until the vinegar reduces by half, about 5 minutes.

Pour in the reserved cooking liquid from braising the shoulder (or stock or water) and bring to a boil. Add the sausage and collard greens and decrease the heat to medium-low. Cover the pot and cook until the greens are tender and silky, about 45 minutes. If the liquid reduces too much, add an additional ½ cup water to the pot.

Remove the sausage from the cooking liquid, cut it into 1-inch-thick slices, and return them to the pot of greens. At this point the greens can be cooled completely and stored for up to 5 days in the refrigerator.

PUT IT TOGETHER AND SERVE Preheat the oven to 350°F. If reheating the pork shoulder, cook, covered, until bubbly and warm in the middle, about 45 minutes. Add the greens and sausage to the pot and continue cooking, uncovered, until the greens and cooking liquid are bubbling and slightly reduced, an additional 20 minutes. (If you're not reheating the pork and making this all in one go, just add the greens and sausage during the last 20 minutes of braising.)

In a medium bowl, toss together the onion, parsley, bread crumbs, lemon juice, oil, and salt. Top the pork and greens with the salad and serve.

BRINED AND BRAISED PORK SHOULDER WITH KNEPFLE NOODLES, CABBAGE, CARAWAY, AND APPLE

Knepfle (pronounced NEFF-la) is the Alsatian version of spaetzle. I got this recipe from Chef Paul Virant, who got it from from Chef Jean Joho. These are less like soft egg noodles and more like little dumplings, and super delicious because they're a little lighter and crisp up in a pan full of butter—which is exactly what you do before dumping them over the top of the pork with some seared charred cabbage and tart green apple.

Knepfle Noodles

1 cup sour cream
1½ cups all-purpose flour
2 eggs
1 teaspoon kosher salt
2 tablespoons extra-virgin olive oil

Charred Cabbage

1 head cabbage (preferably winter white, but good old-fashioned green cabbage works, too)
2 tablespoons extra-virgin olive oil
2 teaspoons kosher salt
1 tablespoon caraway seeds
1 tablespoon poppy seeds
1 tablespoon unsalted butter
Juice of 1 lemon

1 brined and braised pork shoulder (see page 224), in its braising liquid
2 tablespoons unsalted butter
1 tart apple, such as Granny Smith, thinly sliced
½ cup Italian parsley leaves
1 teaspoon freshly squeezed lemon juice
2 teaspoons extra-virgin olive oil
¼ teaspoon kosher salt

MAKE THE NOODLES In a medium bowl, whisk together the sour cream, flour, eggs, and salt until a soft batter forms.

Bring a large pot of salted water to a boil over high heat. Add one-third of the batter to a colander with large holes. Using a rubber spatula, push the batter through the holes into the boiling water. Stir the water to separate the noodles and cook until the noodles float to the surface, 2 to 3 minutes. Use a fine-mesh sieve to scoop the noodles from the water. Drain them well, transfer them to a large metal bowl or baking sheet, and toss with enough of the oil to coat, to keep them from sticking. Repeat until all the batter has been used. The noodles can be stored in the fridge for 1 to 2 days.

continued

BRINED AND BRAISED PORK SHOULDER WITH KNEPFLE NOODLES, CABBAGE, CARAWAY, AND APPLE

continued

CHAR THE CABBAGE Preheat the broiler to high. Slice the cabbage in half through the stem. Cut the cabbage into 1-inch-thick wedges, removing most of the thick core. Coat the wedges in the oil, salt, and caraway and poppy seeds. Arrange the cabbage on a rimmed baking sheet and place it on the oven rack closest to the broiler. Cook until the wedges are charred and beginning to soften, about 7 minutes. Keep an eye on it! Remove the sheet from the oven, dot the cabbage with the butter, and squirt with the lemon juice. Set aside until ready to use or store in the fridge for up to 5 days. If you make it ahead, gently warm the cabbage on a baking sheet in a 350°F oven for 8 to 10 minutes before serving or toss it in with the pork shoulder for the final 10 minutes or so.

PUT IT TOGETHER AND SERVE Preheat the oven to 350°F. If reheating the pork shoulder, cook, covered, until bubbly and warm in the middle, about 45 minutes.

In a large skillet, heat the butter over medium-high heat and allow it to melt and begin to foam. Add the knepfle and cook 6 to 8 minutes, or until the noodles are warmed through and slightly browned. Toss in the cabbage and set aside. You could also just toss the knepfle in with the pork shoulder for the final 10 minutes or so.

In a medium bowl, toss together the apple, parsley, lemon juice, oil, and salt. Top the pork with the cabbage, knepfle, and salad and serve.

233

BRINED AND BRAISED PORK SHOULDER WITH BRAISED APRICOTS, COUSCOUS, AND FENNEL YOGURT

MAKES 6 SERVINGS

I'm crazy about braised dried apricots; they just have this beautiful natural sweetness and tartness. I mean, maybe one in fifty times you get a great fresh apricot, but that might be once every three years. But you can get decent dried apricots anywhere, and if you're lucky enough to get some that still have a little blush to them, like in California where they grow, they're insanely good. I always braise them with a little red wine and then throw them into the pot with the pork at the end of the braise. They also make a great cheese accompaniment and go well with chicken. Or you could cut them into smaller pieces and toss them into the braising liquid that you thicken with a knob of butter and end up with an amazing sauce for steak, chicken, or just about anything else. In this recipe, they're paired with couscous and some doctored-up yogurt for sort of a Moroccan situation. Yogurt is probably one of the most underrated flavor vehicles, adding really nice acidity to a dish. Here, it's just good Greek yogurt or labneh, if you can find it, with some toasted fennel seeds and honey stirred in. Doesn't get easier than that.

Braised Apricots

8 ounces dried apricots
2 tablespoons unsalted butter
1 cup good but cheap red wine
1 teaspoon thyme leaves
½ teaspoon kosher salt

Couscous

1¼ cups water
Extra-virgin olive oil
Kosher salt
1 cup couscous*

Fennel Yogurt

½ cup plain Greek yogurt
2 tablespoons honey
2 teaspoons fennel seeds, toasted in a skillet until aromatic, then ground
¼ teaspoon kosher salt

1 brined and braised pork shoulder (see page 224), in its braising liquid
1 small bulb fennel, thinly sliced
½ cup mint leaves
1 teaspoon freshly squeezed lemon juice
2 teaspoons extra-virgin olive oil
¼ teaspoon kosher salt

235

BRAISE THE APRICOTS In a small saucepan, combine the apricots, butter, red wine, thyme, and salt. Cook over medium-low heat until the wine has reduced and the apricots are plump, 10 to 15 minutes. Set aside until ready to use in this recipe or store in the fridge for up to 5 days.

continued

*I prefer whole-wheat.

BRINED AND BRAISED PORK SHOULDER WITH BRAISED APRICOTS, COUSCOUS, AND FENNEL YOGURT

continued

COOK THE COUSCOUS In a medium pot, bring the water to a boil over medium-high heat. Add a splash of oil and a pinch of salt. Stir in the couscous, remove the pot from the heat, and cover. Let the couscous absorb the liquid and steam for 10 minutes. Set aside until ready to use in this recipe or fluff with a fork and store in the fridge for up to 5 days. To reheat, put the couscous in a fine-mesh strainer over a pot of boiling water, taking care not to let the couscous touch the water. Put a lid on the strainer and steam for 5 minutes, stirring occasionally until warmed through. You could also throw everything in a microwave.

MAKE THE YOGURT In a medium bowl, combine the yogurt, honey, ground fennel, and salt. Set aside until ready to use for this recipe or store in the fridge for up to 5 days.

PUT IT TOGETHER AND SERVE Preheat the oven to 350°F. If reheating the pork shoulder, cook, covered, until bubbly and warm in the middle, about 45 minutes. Add the apricots to the pot and continue cooking, uncovered, until the cooking liquid is bubbling and slightly reduced, an additional 20 minutes. (If you're not reheating the pork and making this all in one go, just add the apricots during the last 20 minutes of braising.) Remove the pot from the oven and add the couscous to the cooking liquid.

In a medium bowl, toss together the fennel, mint, lemon juice, oil, and salt. Top the pork with the yogurt and salad and serve.

236

BRINED AND BRAISED PORK SHOULDER WITH FRESH PEAS, SAFFRON ORZO, AND CLAMS

MAKES 6 SERVINGS

PICTURED ON PAGES 238 AND 239. This is like springtime on some Greek island. It's bright and briny from the clams, is fresh from the peas, and gets great golden color from the saffron (which also adds a sort of funky acidity that rounds out the whole dish). It's proof that you can take something heavier like a pork braise and make it lighter for warmer weather.

Saffron Orzo
Pinch of saffron
2 tablespoons kosher salt
1 pound orzo

1 brined and braised pork shoulder
(see page 224), in its braising
liquid
1 pound shucked fresh peas
(about 3 pounds in the pod)
or frozen peas

1 pound littleneck clams
1 (12-ounce) jar olive oil–marinated
artichoke hearts; or 1½ cups from
the salad bar in the fancy grocery
stores; or 1 small red onion, thinly
sliced, plus 1 tablespoon extra-
virgin olive oil
½ cup Italian parsley leaves
1 teaspoon freshly squeezed
lemon juice
¼ teaspoon kosher salt

MAKE THE ORZO In a large saucepan, bring 3 quarts of water plus the saffron and salt to a boil over high heat. Add the orzo and cook for 7 minutes. Drain the pasta and set aside until ready to use for this recipe or in the fridge for up to 5 days.

PUT IT TOGETHER AND SERVE Preheat the oven to 350°F. If reheating the pork shoulder, cook, covered, until bubbly and warm in the middle, about 45 minutes. Add the orzo, peas, and clams to the pot and continue cooking, uncovered, for an additional 10 to 15 minutes, or until the clams have opened and the cooking liquid is bubbling and slightly reduced. Discard any clams that have not opened.

In a medium bowl, toss together the artichoke hearts, parsley, lemon juice, and salt. Top the pork and orzo with the fresh salad and serve.

237

12

A lot of people think grilling is the way to go when it comes to steak, and while I'm not going to tell someone to *not* fire up a grill, I can tell you that searing a great piece of meat just takes it to a whole other level. A great sear in a ripping-hot pan not only gives you that nice crust, but it's also rendering off the steak's fat, which is super-flavorful and ultimately becomes what the meat is cooking in. I also add a little butter to the pan, especially when cooking a leaner cut that isn't kicking off any of its own fat (which we'll talk more about in a bit). It's not totally necessary and you could opt out of it, but it makes for a damn tasty steak. Same with adding some garlic and thyme to the pan. I'll never forget the time Jonathan Waxman stayed at our cabin and he was like, "Pablo, how should we cook the steak tonight? Grill or sear it in a pan?" To which I said: "Sear it in pan." The whole house filled up with smoke because we didn't have proper ventilation yet, but it was hands-down the best steak ever.

And by the way, if you're cooking a steak that can (safely) stand on its fatty side without falling over and splashing you with hot oil, that crispy bit of fat is really special—it's what we call a *schnoogan*, named after the mythical god of deliciousness, Jimmy Schnoogan. You can thank my chef friend Brian Huston for this bit of nonsense.

COOK A STEAK, ANY STEAK

To Drink

Bring in the big guns: full-bodied, full-fruit reds like Primitivo or Sicilian Nero d'Avola, or Moroccan reds, which are full of spice, have less oak, and are less expensive. Even though it's classic to go with Barolo or California Cabernet, it's just not my style.

here's how

PICK A STEAK, MARINATE, SEAR, BASTE, AND FINISH

Some of these cuts will be closer to 1 pound in the butcher case, others will weigh in at 2 pounds. This recipe will work whether you're cooking two 1-pound steaks or one 2-pound steak, regardless of the cut. (Just be sure to adjust for the slightly different cooking times.)

MAKES 6 SERVINGS

2 (1-pound) hunks or 1 (2-pound) hunk of beef: flap steak, flank, hanger, New York strip, rib eye, tenderloin, or tri-tip
2 teaspoons kosher salt
1 teaspoon freshly ground black pepper
1 cup Tasty Meat Marinade #1 or #2 (page 138; optional)
¼ cup rice bran, grapeseed, or pure olive oil (save the extra-virgin for finishing)
4 cloves garlic, smashed in their peels
1 small bunch thyme
¼ cup unsalted butter
½ teaspoon good, flaky sea salt
2 teaspoons extra-virgin olive oil

Pick a Steak

First, consider your options from the seven different cuts, from least to most expensive and, incidentally, in order of my preference.

FLAP: This is what's called "butcher steak," as in, it's what the butcher wants to stash under the counter to take home himself. It comes from the bottom sirloin, varies from pretty thin to about 2 inches thick, and is actually surprisingly well marbled. Other than rib eye, it's probably got the most fat, and it makes for great richness and flavor. The key for cooking flap, more so than any other steak, is letting it rest for a full 10 minutes after cooking because it will really bleed out a lot of juice if you don't. I also don't think it should be cooked more than medium-rare or medium. It tends to lose all its juice if you cook it too much.

FLANK: This is basically from the same part of the animal as flap but a little more forward toward the belly flap. It also maxes out around 2 inches thick and is similar in flavor and texture to flap steak.

HANGER: Another butcher's cut, this time from the diaphragm. It weighs a pound to a pound and a half, and you have to marinate it or else it's really tough. But after that, it has super-beefy flavor.

NEW YORK STRIP, RIB EYE, TENDERLOIN: These are all similarly priced, though tenderloin (which I'm including slightly under protest, even though it can be really good and is widely available) tends to go up in price around the holidays. Tenderloin has the least fat and really benefits from a super-hard sear and a baste with butter. Rib eye would be the steak-eaters' favorite. It has a current of fat that runs from small to very large, so you can pick a steak that has what you're looking for. Strips are pretty consistent from end to end and have a medium amount of fat (between what you'd find in a tenderloin and a rib eye). Both the strip and the rib eye you can find bone-in, though for ease of use we call for boneless because it's more difficult to cook bone-in evenly (it tends to be a little more rare around the bone) and to slice. But then again, the bones help retain flavor and juiciness, so it can be worth the extra effort. None of these steaks needs a marinade—I would just go with salt and pepper.

TRI-TIP: This is a big thing in Northern California, Tex-Mex cooking, and also in Argentina. It's another cut from the bottom sirloin area and is kinda related to the flap steak. It's pretty affordable and also a nice size to grill. It benefits from a marinade for both flavor and texture. The tricky part with a tri-tip—because it's a primal cut—is that it has more than one muscle running through it. So you might end up with a chewier piece if you're not cutting across the grain.

continued

244

OTHER THINGS TO THINK ABOUT WHEN BUYING A STEAK: If you like a more well-done steak, stick with strip or rib eye because they'll still be juicy. Other cuts'll just dry out. From a flavor standpoint, pastured meat that's finished on grain is a favorite of mine. And if you have the opportunity to know the farmer who raised the animals, that's important and helpful, too.

Marinate (if you want)

One hour before you're ready to cook the steak, remove it from the fridge. This will allow the meat to shake off some of the chill from the fridge so the steak will cook more quickly and evenly. Decide at this point if you want to marinate it. Prime cuts, like the rib eye and New York strip, won't need it for tenderizing purposes, but the flavor doesn't hurt. The tri-tip, flank, hanger, and flap can all use a little help in the tenderizing department.

IF YOU DO NOT MARINATE: (1) Season the steak with kosher salt and pepper on all sides and allow it to rest for 1 hour at room temperature.

IF YOU DO MARINATE: Season the steak with kosher salt and pepper on all sides and then submerge in the marinade and let sit for 1 hour at room temperature.

Sear

Preheat the oven 375°F. Heat a large ovenproof skillet (bonus points for using cast iron) over medium-high heat. (2) Add the rice bran, grapeseed, or pure olive oil and continue to heat until it shimmers and easily glides across the pan. Turn down the heat just a tick—you want high heat but you don't want to burn down the house. (3) Carefully add the steak to the pan. Let the steak sear undisturbed for 4 minutes if cooking two smaller steaks, 7 minutes for one larger steak. Lift one corner of the steak to see if a nice, golden brown crust has formed. If the steak lifts easily from the pan and there is good color, use tongs or a meat fork to flip the steak, taking care not to splatter yourself with the hot oil. (4) Allow the second side to sear for 4 to 7 minutes, again depending on the size, or until it lifts easily from the pan and has a nice crust.

Baste and Finish in the Oven

(5) Add the garlic, thyme, and butter to the pan. It will sputter and smell delicious. (6) As the butter melts, use a large spoon to ladle the butter over the top of the steak. Baste repeatedly for about 30 seconds. You can carefully tip the pan toward you so the butter pools and makes it easier to spoon from. Transfer the pan to the oven.

If cooking two smaller steaks, cook for 4 minutes. If cooking one larger steak, cook for 8 minutes. Remove the steak from the oven, flip it in the pan, and baste it a few times. Take its temperature with a meat thermometer—you're looking for 130°F or a couple degrees lower or higher, depending on your doneness preference. If it's not quite there, baste the steak again before returning it to the oven to cook for a couple minutes more.

Rest

(7) Remove the steak from the pan and transfer it to a cooling rack set over a baking sheet. Let it rest for at least 10 minutes, but 15 to 20 minutes is even better if you can wait that long. During this time, the steak will come up another 10 degrees to hit medium doneness, and it will also relax and redistribute its juices. Be patient—it's worth it to not have your juices run out of your steak.

Slice and Serve

(8, 9) Slice the steak into ¼- to ½-inch-thick slices. For a rib eye or New York strip, it doesn't matter as much which direction you slice. For other cuts, pay attention to the grain of the steak (the direction that the muscle runs). For a more tender steak on the plate, you want to cut against the grain with your knife at a slight angle.

Arrange the sliced steak on a large platter, pour over any remaining juices from the cutting board, and finish with the sea salt and extra-virgin olive oil.

STEAK WITH CHARRED RADICCHIO, HONEY-ROASTED SQUASH, AND PEPITA PESTO

MAKES 6 SERVINGS

I'd been oven- and pan-roasting squash forever and then saw in some healthy cooking magazine a Michel Nischan recipe with honey, olive oil, and salt—all tossed with some acorn squash with the skin on. It was so simple and really delicious, especially the way the skin gets all roasty and caramelized. I serve this with charred radicchio, and also squash seeds (technically pumpkin seeds) that are turned into a pesto instead of using the usual pine nuts. It's a total fall dish.

Honey-Roasted Squash

1 pound winter squash (about
    1 medium butternut, 2 delicata,
    or 2 acorn squash)
2 tablespoons extra-virgin olive oil
2 tablespoons honey
1 teaspoon kosher salt
1 teaspoon thyme leaves*
¼ teaspoon freshly ground
    black pepper

Pepita Pesto

½ cup raw pumpkin seeds
    (aka pepitas)
½ cup grated Parmigiano cheese
½ cup extra-virgin olive oil
3 cloves garlic, peeled
2 cups Italian parsley leaves
½ teaspoon kosher salt

Charred Radicchio

¼ cup balsamic vinegar
2 tablespoons honey
2 heads radicchio, cored and cut
    into ½-inch slices
1 teaspoon kosher salt, plus more
    as needed
6 cranks black pepper
2 tablespoons extra-virgin olive oil,
    plus more as needed
Juice of 1 lemon

1 steak of choice (see page 244),
    cooked, rested, and warm

248

*Bonus points for including, but not necessary if you don't have it handy.

MAKE THE SQUASH Preheat the oven 350°F. Slice off the top(s) and bottom(s) of the squash, cut in half, and scoop out the seeds. No need to peel! Cut the meat into ¼-inch-wide slices.

Toss the squash onto a rimmed baking sheet and add the oil, honey, salt, thyme, and pepper and stir around until the squash is evenly coated. Roast for 8 minutes, or until the squash starts to sizzle. Stir everything around again and return the pan to the oven for 5 minutes more. Keep checking and stirring every 5 minutes until the squash is golden brown and tender but not falling apart, 20 to 25 minutes total. Set aside.

MAKE THE PESTO In a blender, combine the pumpkin seeds, cheese, oil, and garlic and blend until smooth. Add the parsley and salt and blend just until the parsley is pureed (this helps keep the color a little brighter green). Set aside until ready to serve or store in the fridge for up to 5 days. It'll lose some of its color as it sits, but it will still taste delicious.

CHAR THE RADICCHIO In a small bowl, whisk together the vinegar and honey. In a large bowl, toss together the radicchio, vinegar mixture, salt, and pepper.

Heat the oil in a large, heavy-bottomed sauté pan over high heat until the oil shimmers and is almost smoking. Carefully drain off the vinegar mixture into a small bowl, save it, and add the radicchio to the pan. Cook it on one side until it's deeply charred, 4 to 5 minutes. You may need to do this in two batches, adding more oil to the pan if necessary. Transfer the radicchio to a clean bowl, decrease the heat to medium-low, and add the reserved vinegar mixture to the pan. Reduce it until it's slightly thickened, about 2 minutes. Add the reduced vinegar and half of the lemon juice to the charred radicchio, toss, and taste. It might need a pinch of salt or a squeeze more of lemon.

PUT IT TOGETHER AND SERVE Cut the steak and arrange the pieces on a serving platter. Scatter the squash and radicchio around the meat, spoon the pesto over the top, and serve. Alternatively, serve the steak, squash, and radicchio on separate platters.

STEAK WITH ROASTED LEEKS AND ANCHOVY BUTTER

MAKES 6 SERVINGS

Your average person doesn't think of meat and anchovies going together, but anchovies' code name is umami. You don't taste the fish; it's just like the sixth unknown taste. Savoriness and salt. And while being a fat-on-fat chef isn't my MO, there's something about grilled steak and butter that's a no-brainer. It just carries the flavor more, especially if it's not on a super-duper fatty cut of meat, such as tenderloin. While you could use any kind of onion here, leeks are underrated. If you cook them down and char them up a little bit, they get sweet. And if you can roast them until they're tender and then toss them in the pan with a steak that's giving up all its fat so the leeks char a little bit—I'd say that's a pretty good bet.

Anchovy Butter
¼ cup oil-packed salted anchovies
¼ cup red wine vinegar
2 small shallots, minced
1 cup unsalted butter, softened
½ cup chopped Italian parsley leaves

Roasted Leeks
3 pounds leeks, roots and dark
  green tops trimmed off
1 teaspoon salt
½ cup dry white wine*
2 tablespoons unsalted butter
2 tablespoons extra-virgin olive oil
  (optional)

1 steak of choice (see page 244),
  cooked, rested, and warm

251

MAKE THE ANCHOVY BUTTER In a small saucepan, combine the anchovies, vinegar, and shallots. Cook over medium heat for about 5 minutes, or until the vinegar is completely reduced and the shallots are soft.

In a medium bowl, combine the shallot mixture, butter, and parsley and stir to combine. Keep the butter at room temperature if you are using it right away; otherwise it can be refrigerated for 5 days or frozen for 1 month. Just return the butter to room temperature before using.

COOK THE LEEKS Split the leeks in half lengthwise and then rinse well.

Preheat the oven to 350°F. Place the leeks on a small rimmed baking sheet or in an ovenproof pan in a single layer, cut-side down. Season with the salt and add the wine, butter, and oil to the pan. Roast until the leeks are tender when pierced with a knife, about 20 minutes. Set aside until ready to serve or store in the refrigerator for up to 5 days.

When the steak has 10 minutes left to cook, add the roasted leeks to the pan and cook until they're nicely charred, about 10 minutes. Alternatively, cook the leeks in a separate pan over high heat with the olive oil. Or drop them, cut-side down, on a preheated grill. Cut the leeks in half the short way to serve.

PUT IT TOGETHER AND SERVE Cut the steak and arrange it on a serving platter. Schmear half of the anchovy butter on top of the slices, scatter the leeks over the platter, and serve the rest of the butter on the side (any leftover butter is great on vegetables, like green beans and broccoli).

*I like to use Sauvignon Blanc or something else with good acidity.

STEAK WITH HERBY HUMMUS, ASPARAGUS, AND CHARRED SCALLIONS

MAKES 6 SERVINGS

It's a long, dreadful winter here in Chicago, so I'm stacking the deck with all of spring's greatest hits. All green, all spring.

Herby Hummus

1 recipe Cheater Hummus (page 35)
    or 2 cups store-bought hummus
½ bunch Italian parsley, leaves only
2 scallions (white and green parts),
    coarsely chopped

2 bunches asparagus, woody ends
    snapped off
1 bunch scallions or spring onions
2 cloves garlic, unpeeled

¾ cup extra-virgin olive oil
1½ teaspoons kosher salt
2 tablespoons chopped dill leaves
Zest and juice of 1 lemon
¼ teaspoon crushed red chile flakes

1 steak of choice (see page 244),
    cooked, rested, and warm

MAKE THE HUMMUS Add the Cheater Hummus, parsley, and scallions to a blender and blend until smooth. Set aside until ready to use or store in the fridge for up to 5 days.

BROIL THE VEG Preheat the broiler to high. In a shallow baking pan or rimmed baking sheet, combine the asparagus, scallions or spring onions, and garlic. Keep everything separate and in one layer as much as possible. Drizzle with ½ cup of the oil and 1 teaspoon of the salt. Place the pan under the broiler and cook until the scallions are charred in spots and are soft, about 5 minutes. Remove the scallions and garlic from the pan and turn the asparagus. Return to the broiler and cook until the asparagus is tender and a bit charred, about another 5 minutes.

PUT IT TOGETHER AND SERVE While the asparagus is cooking, coarsely chop the scallions and peel and slice the garlic. Toss them in a medium bowl with the remaining ½ teaspoon salt, the dill, lemon zest and juice, and the chile flakes. Whisk in the remaining ¼ cup oil. Schmear a bed of hummus on a serving platter and top with the asparagus and sliced steak. Spoon the charred scallion vinaigrette over the top.

253

COOK A STEAK, ANY STEAK

STEAK WITH WALNUT TAPENADE, GREEN OLIVES, AND FRESH HORSERADISH

Another springtime-y combo, this time with a coarse tapenade featuring chunks of walnuts and olive, almost like an olive salad. A real hand-chopper kind of deal. I like Castelvetranos here, but any kind of meaty, not-too-salty variety of olive would be great. For me, the real star is the freshly grated horseradish over the whole thing because it adds a super-bright pungency. You can find fresh horseradish root pretty much year-round, and most grocery stores have it wrapped in plastic in the refrigerated case near the produce. It's kind of like plutonium—it doesn't go bad. And in case it doesn't go without saying, this is not the time for jarred. The only time for jarred is in cocktail sauce, specifically for shrimp cocktail, one of the great culinary inventions.

Walnut Tapenade

½ cup fresh English peas, or frozen peas in a pinch (or sugar snap peas, shelled and peeled fava beans, or even diced celery)
Kosher salt
½ cup walnut pieces, toasted in a skillet until aromatic
½ cup Castelvetrano olives, pitted and coarsely chopped

¼ bunch Italian parsley, leaves only
¼ cup extra-virgin olive oil
1 tablespoon freshly squeezed lemon juice
Pinch of red chile flakes

1 steak of choice (see page 244), cooked, rested, and warm
1 (1-inch) piece horseradish root, rough outer skin peeled

255

MAKE THE TAPENADE If you are using fresh peas, you'll need to cook them briefly. If you use frozen peas, just let them thaw at room temperature for 15 minutes before using. (No need to cook the sugar snap peas, favas, or celery, if using.) To cook the fresh peas, bring 1 quart water with 2 table-spoons salt to a boil in a medium saucepan over high heat. Add the fresh peas all at once and cook for 30 seconds. Drain the peas and transfer them to a medium bowl. Add the walnuts, olives, parsley, oil, lemon juice, chile flakes, and ½ teaspoon salt. Stir well to combine and taste; it might need a pinch more salt if the olives aren't very salty.

PUT IT TOGETHER AND SERVE Cut the steak and arrange on a serving platter. Spoon the tapenade over the sliced steak. Using a rasp grater, grate the horseradish over the top of everything and serve.

STEAK WITH CHARRED TOMATOES AND BURNT EGGPLANT

MAKES 6 SERVINGS

And now for summertime. When I say "burnt eggplant," it's real-deal burnt. We're talking black, collapsed, and flattened. Then it gets thrown in the blender with tahini, lemon juice, and olive oil—skin and all. Many people will tell you to peel the eggplant first, but there's a lot of great smoky, charry flavor there that you don't want to throw away. As for the tomatoes, this is pretty much the standard One-Off Hospitality roasted-tomato recipe that we use across all our restaurants. It's so simple and good and the juice left on the bottom of the pan is . . . invaluable. That's where all the action is, so don't forget to pour it over your steak.

Charred Tomatoes

1 pound cherry tomatoes*
2 tablespoons extra-virgin olive oil
1 teaspoon kosher salt

Burnt Eggplant

2 pounds Japanese eggplant
¼ cup tahini
2 tablespoons freshly squeezed
lemon juice

2 tablespoons extra-virgin olive oil
1 teaspoon kosher salt
6 big cranks black pepper
½ teaspoon ground cumin
¼ teaspoon crushed red chile flakes

1 steak of choice (see page 244),
cooked, rested, and warm
Small bunch basil, leaves torn
2 tablespoons extra-virgin olive oil

256

CHAR THE TOMATOES Preheat the oven 375°F. (This is the same temp that the steak will cook at, so you can do this at the same time.)

Toss together the tomatoes, oil, and salt in a shallow rimmed baking sheet. Roast until the tomatoes are tender and starting to pop, 10 minutes.

COOK THE EGGPLANT Preheat the broiler or light a grill. If using a broiler, place the eggplant (whole . . . don't cut it) in a shallow rimmed baking sheet and place it as close to the flame as you can get it. Otherwise, just put it directly on the grill grate. Cook the eggplant until it is very dark and charred on the top (we call it "burnt eggplant" for a reason; don't be shy), 5 to 10 minutes. Rotate the eggplant and repeat. Continue to cook until the eggplant is completely charred and starting to collapse, another 5 to 10 minutes. So, char, rotate, repeat.

Let the eggplant cool slightly. Cut off just the stem end and place the whole eggplant in a blender with the tahini, lemon juice, oil, salt, pepper, cumin, and chile flakes. Blend on high speed until smooth. Set aside until ready to serve or store in the fridge for up to 5 days.

PUT IT TOGETHER AND SERVE Schmear the burnt eggplant on a large platter. Cut the steak and arrange over the eggplant. Top with the tomatoes and their pan juices, the torn basil leaves, and the oil, and serve.

*Bonus points if you can find them on the stem.

13

When I'm cooking at home and serving dessert, I want to be able to just pull something out of the fridge and be done with it. I don't want anything I need to cut a certain way, whip any cream for, or even scoop, like ice cream. There's nothing fussy about these two desserts (developed by Dana Cree, formerly the pastry chef at Blackbird and Publican and a hands-down dessert genius), which are both really simple and are essentially blank canvases for fruit in all its various forms (poached, roasted, as is). Posset is an old English dessert that's based on cream and sugar. It's sort of like panna cotta, except it's a little more dense and like a pudding, and it doesn't wobble when it hits the table. Yet, it's bright and clean, thanks to a little bit of lemon, which is what's traditionally used to curdle the cream. It's also super-easy to make, but super-impressive. The olive oil cake initially was developed for avec and was perfect because we could just pick it up on the line, throw it in the oven for a few minutes until it got slightly caramelized and oily (in a good way), and then serve it with fruit.

MAKE A SIMPLE DESSERT

To Drink

Look for something that has a little bit of sweetness but isn't too sweet—a sweeter amaro, a sweeter sherry, and lighter fortified reds (like Madeira or Port). Personally, I'd go for a nice glass of brown liquor, like whiskey or a beautiful aged rum. Or just finish off what you've got left in the bottles on the table.

POSSET

This can be made in a single dish (that holds up to 6 cups) or in six individual vessels: small bowls, ramekins, casuelas, coffee cups . . . just make sure that they each hold 1 cup of liquid.

½ cup buttermilk
¼ cup plus 3 tablespoons freshly
    squeezed lemon juice
1 sheet of gelatin
4¼ cups heavy cream

1 cup sugar
1 teaspoon lemon zest
1 pint berries of choice,
    or 3 nectarines, pitted
    and sliced

BLOOM THE GELATIN In a small bowl, combine the buttermilk, lemon juice, and gelatin. Set aside.

MAKE THE POSSET In a medium saucepan, combine the heavy cream, sugar, and lemon zest. Bring to a boil over medium-high heat, stirring occasionally with a rubber spatula to ensure that the cream does not scorch. Decrease the heat to medium-low to prevent the cream from boiling over and continue to boil for 5 minutes, stirring occasionally. Remove the pot from the heat and add the gelatin mixture. Stir well and let the mixture sit at room temperature for 10 minutes. Pour the mixture into your serving dish(es) of choice. Chill in the fridge, covered, overnight.

ADD THE FRUIT AND SERVE Spoon the berries over the serving dish(es) and serve. Store leftover posset in the fridge for up to 3 days.

OLIVE OIL CAKE

**MAKES 6 SERVINGS (WITH SOME
LEFTOVERS . . . MAYBE)**

This cake is really versatile, holds up well (it stays moist forever because of all the olive oil in it), and can be either seared in a pan or served at room temp.

Macerated Fruit Topping

1 pound fruit (raspberries, blackberries, sliced strawberries, peaches, plums, nectarines, halved cherries)
2 to 4 tablespoons sugar
Zest and juice of ½ lemon

or

Cooked Fruit Topping #1

1 pound fruit (raspberries, blackberries, blueberries, sliced peaches, strawberries, plums, nectarines, halved cherries)
2 to 4 tablespoons sugar
Zest and juice of ½ lemon

or

Cooked Fruit Topping #2

¼ cup unsalted butter
1 pound apples or pears, peeled, cored, and sliced into ¼-inch wedges
¼ cup sugar
½ teaspoon ground cinnamon
1 teaspoon vanilla extract, or seeds from ½ vanilla bean

continued

Olive Oil Cake

1 tablespoon unsalted butter, melted, plus more for greasing
1 cup plus 1 tablespoon all-purpose flour
¾ cup sugar
1 teaspoon baking soda
¼ teaspoon kosher salt
½ cup plus 2 tablespoons buttermilk
¼ cup sour cream
1 egg
¼ cup plus 1 tablespoon extra-virgin olive oil
2 tablespoons plus 2 teaspoons hot water

MAKE A SIMPLE DESSERT

OLIVE OIL CAKE

continued

MAKE A TOPPING If making the macerated topping, combine the fruit, 2 tablespoons of the sugar, and the lemon zest and juice in a medium bowl. Stir to coat well, and taste. Add an additional 1 to 2 tablespoons sugar, depending on the tartness of your fruit. Let rest at room temperature for at least 30 minutes before serving, or refrigerate for up to 4 hours, bringing the mixture back to room temperature before serving.

If making cooked fruit topping #1, combine the fruit, 2 to 4 tablespoons sugar (depending on the tartness of your fruit), and the lemon zest and juice in a medium saucepan. Cook over low heat, stirring occasionally, until the fruit gives off its own juice and the sauce thickens slightly, about 10 minutes. Set aside until ready to serve or store in the fridge for up to 5 days.

If making cooked fruit topping #2, melt the butter over low heat in a medium saucepan. Add the apples or pears, sugar, cinnamon, and vanilla and stir well to coat the fruit. Cover the pan and cook, stirring occasionally, until the fruit is soft and just starting to caramelize, about 10 minutes. Serve warm, straight from the pan. Store leftover topping in the fridge for up to 5 days.

PREP THE PAN Preheat the oven to 325°F. Generously grease an 8-inch cake pan or cast-iron skillet with butter and set aside.

MAKE THE CAKE BATTER In the bowl of a stand mixer fitted with the paddle attachment, combine the flour, sugar, baking soda, and salt. Set aside.

In a mixing bowl, combine the buttermilk, sour cream, and egg and whisk to blend well. Set aside.

In a small bowl, combine the oil and melted butter. Set aside.

Mix the dry ingredients on low speed to combine. Add the dairy, mix to combine, and scrape down the bowl with a rubber spatula. Add the oil-butter mixture, mix to combine, and scrape down the bowl again. Add the hot water and mix until just combined.

BAKE THE CAKE Pour the batter into the prepared pan and bake for 35 minutes, or until golden brown and a toothpick comes out clean when inserted in the middle. Let the cake cool in the pan for 10 minutes. Run a knife around the inside of the pan to loosen the cake and then turn it out onto a cooling rack. Store, well wrapped, at room temperature for up to 2 days.

TOP AND SERVE Top with your topping of choice and serve.

AFTERWORD

270

It's coincidental that the project that ended up setting the stage for avec is one that never actually came to life. In the mid-'90s, two years before my business partners—Paul Kahan and Rick Diarmit—and I opened our first restaurant, Blackbird, we were looking at a space on Milwaukee Avenue in Chicago with designer Thomas Schlesser. We wanted to open a restaurant called Table, with a single communal dining table right in the center of the room.

The dining room at Blackbird doesn't have communal seating, but the tables are so close together, you can still feel the sort of intimacy that comes from enjoying a meal with relative strangers. We never did end up opening Table, but the idea for that restaurant, combined with what we'd observed in the early days of Blackbird, got us all thinking about how to create community and family around a dining table that exists outside the home.

The feeling we were after was one of warm familiarity, and, naturally, that took us to Europe. In the fall of 2003, avec's opening Chef de Cuisine Koren Grieveson traveled to France with Rick and me. We

were there for inspiration; to experience the restaurants that had been doing communal dining before it was called that, which is where Benoit comes in. Benoit is a little one–Michelin star restaurant that's been in business for more than one hundred years. The space is super-tight; the tables can't be more than 4 inches apart. It reminded us of Blackbird, and we started to wonder what would happen if we pushed the tables together. We decided to take a shot at turning 24 x 30-inch tables into 96 x 30-inch ones, and avec was born, with five long communal tables.

That was fifteen years ago. The country was fragile in the wake of September 11, and having dinner at a big table in a small restaurant felt like a source of security rather than an ordeal. We opened avec with Koren as the chef, under Paul's mentorship and through the lens of his own travels across Spain, Italy, and France. They were cooking in an open kitchen, and Eduard Seitan was our wine steward.

I'll admit it wasn't perfect. In the beginning, it was difficult to get people to sit in the middle section of the communals. Everybody wanted to post up on the ends, so it was kind of like playing Tetris. Gradually, that changed. We loved watching people ask one another, "Excuse me, but what are you eating?" and the reply being, "Those are the dates. Would you like to try some?" I mean, where else does that happen? When we think about it, we like to believe that some wonderful conversations, and even a few bonds that extended past those small instances, grew from the words exchanged between neighbors at avec.

It is French for "with," after all.

**—DONNIE MADIA GIANFRANCISCO,
partner, One Off Hospitality**

ACKNOWLEDGMENTS

Our sincerest thanks goes to Mary, Stephanie, Avery, Debbie, Eduard Koren, Jorge, Sontra, Giulietta, all the crews past and present at avec, Donnie, Thomas and Claire, Verena and the people of Gais (Switzerland), Mary and Robert, Aline, Janis, Rachel, Peden + Munk, Jan, Lorena, Lizzie, and the crew at Ten Speed Press.

INDEX

277